T0100285

THE CIVILIZING DISCOURSE

Also by Evan Jones

POETRY

Later Emperors
Paralogues
Nothing Fell Today but Rain

TRANSLATION

The Barbarians Arrive Today:
Poems and Prose of C.P. Cavafy

The Civilizing Discourse

INTERVIEWS WITH CANADIAN POETS

Evan Jones

Véhicule Press

Published with the generous assistance of the Canada Council for the Arts and the Canada Book Fund of the Department of Canadian Heritage.

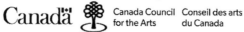

Canada Council   Conseil des arts
for the Arts   du Canada

Cover design by David Drummond
Set in Minion by Simon Garamond
Printed by Livres Rapido Books

Dépôt légal, Library and Archives Canada and the Bibliothèque national du Québec, second trimester 2024

Library and Archives Canada Cataloguing in Publication

Title: The civilizing discourse : interviews with
Canadian poets / Evan Jones.
Names: Jones, Evan, 1973- author.
Identifiers: Canadiana (print) 20240324889 | Canadiana (ebook)
20240324897 | ISBN 9781550656640
(softcover) |ISBN 9781550656664 (EPUB)
Subjects: CSH: Poets, Canadian (English)—20th century—
Biography. | CSH: Poets, Canadian (English)—
20th century—Interviews. | CSH: Poets, Canadian
(English)—21st century—Biography. | CSH: Poets,
Canadian (English)—21st century—Interviews.
| LCGFT: Essays. | LCGFT: Interviews.
Classification: LCC PS8081.1 .J66 2024 | DDC C811/.5409—dc23

Published by Véhicule Press, Montréal, Québec, Canada
www.vehiculepress.com

Distribution in Canada by LitDistCo
www.litdistco.ca

Distribution in US by Independent Publishers Group
www.ipgbook.com

Printed in Canada

For Daryl, Don, Elise, and Steve

Contents

Introduction

This project began when I had more time. And perhaps poetry did too. I was working with Daryl Hine, editing his collections. Daryl, in his role as editor of *Poetry* in the 1970s, had published work by Michael Schmidt, and they were known to each other. Schmidt suggested that I interview Daryl for his journal, *PN Review*. Daryl liked the idea, and there I was, interviewing a poet.

That first interview is a bit all-encompassing, looking at it now. I wanted to position Daryl as best I could and talk about his career. I wish I focused more on his poems. Daryl was sometimes frustrated with the process—he had little interest in going over things he had covered elsewhere. Alongside that, I was writing a PhD and trying to find my own way. We had interests that didn't always coincide. *Poetry* was the loudest, wealthiest, most interesting take at the time, and I wanted Daryl's connection to be clear. But that is a part of his story, not the centre. We managed to get through it together, and a friendship developed out of it. We grew used to exchanging emails regularly, and before long, he asked if I would act as his executor.

Next, I helped to edit an anthology. That process took a good year or two of my life. I put a lot into it. It was widely reviewed and picked at and over. I wanted to reinforce some of its themes by speaking to the poets I had anthologized, making it clear I was not alone in my thinking. The interviews with Norm Sibum, Marius Kociejowski, and Don Coles went quickly, agreeably. I read their work, and we talked. It felt fulfilling to work in my own way with these poets I admired. I spoke to an editor—thank you, Carmine—who expressed interest in a book of interviews like the ones I was doing. All seemed in order.

Then Elise Partridge. She was reticent and, I found out later, going through chemotherapy while we talked. I would send questions and wait months for answers. The process slowed down. The same happened with Steven Heighton—for different reasons. He was working on a variety of projects, was someone who supported himself by his writing, and gave my questions time when he could. Both interviews took over a year to complete, one at a time. I made a note of the start dates, as you'll see, but the process went on so long that it felt strange to include end dates. In both saddening cases, there is one now.

Over that time, my interest in what the anthology represented, and my interests in poetry, changed. Still, I spoke to poets, singly and attentively, if less frequently: Sarah, Moritz, Bringhurst, Compton, Matuk, Mersal. I worked slowly towards the book project. These are poets whose work I read and who I wanted to talk to. In recent years, my concerns have become more formal, less thematic, more process-oriented than biographical—even as those elements play a role in the discussions that follow. I am interested in poets whose works travel. I am interested in poetic form—though not necessarily the formal. I am not very interested in the amateur (I can admire the love that goes into the work), the fashionable (fashion will change), the regional (it is hard work to love that hometown clock tower), the avant-garde (experiment is important but name calling is not).

The interview process is one of the interviewer trying to pin the poet down—and the poet dodging the pins. I would have an idea about a poem or a theme, I would pose that idea as a question, and the poet would shoot me down. Or begin with—worse—a "Yes, but…" Sometimes my questions were aimed at getting poets to explain to me what I could not understand. Sometimes I wanted opposition to my own ideas. Formally—by which I mean the form the interviews took on—I was influenced by the work I did with Anne Compton on her book of interviews, *Meetings with Maritime Poets* (2006). Anne's process was to read everything, to interview in person, and to include the dynamism of the spoken conversation. This latter bit is something, mostly because of distance, I did not have access to. Part of the problem with the email interview is that there is no room for the off-the-cuff remark of the live space. My interviewees had time to think over and edit their responses. And I always sent proofs, meaning that edits could happen at any stage—and did. But that is true of the interview format, anyway—or should be—as editing was ongoing for myself and the interviewee.

So emails were exchanged. This became part of the process even as it was a source of frustration—sometimes on both sides. It was easy enough to adjust to slowness, misreading, and impatience. There was, at times, disagreement. It is not that I sought agreement but that I was trying in my way to connect. But perhaps I went looking to be contradicted. I wanted Steven Heighton to sell me on Al Purdy. I am not, decidedly, in any way, an admirer, and the poem Heighton quotes does not convince me (the sound he admires I find overwrought). But I could, within our discussion, understand the appeal to Heighton and his work. And this is important. The separation now, looking back at these interviews, between myself and the poets seems astonishing. I am amazed we got anywhere in our discussions. But we did, because the answers the poets gave astonished me—they arrived, etymologically, "out of the thunder" of their thinking and work.

An important book for me is Edouard Roditi's *Dialogues: Conversations with European Artists at Mid-Century* (1990). I bought it remaindered at David Mirvish Books on Markham Street decades ago (Toronto has not recovered from the loss of this bookstore), then lost it in a house fire and found another copy. Roditi's book is more in-person than I could manage, and there is so much of his presence. He frames every interview, sometimes interjects with details of his meeting with the artist, explains what they are looking at while they talk. It becomes so much about the two people together, where my instinct is to step away and let the interviewee talk. But what stands out most in Roditi is a vision of the European artworld different from what was happening in the various mainstreams. Roditi speaks to men and women over the course of their careers. Imagine interviewing the German expressionist painter Gabrièle Münter in 1958—not at the peak of her fame but near the end of her life. The book locates a range and vitality outside of the fashionable centres and eras of art.

Of course, my own preoccupations come through. Canadian nationalism and nation building have done their damage. For a long time, to paraphrase Michael Schmidt, people wrote Canadian poems rather than poems. I do not know what space these will occupy in time before us or even in my own lifetime. Some will surely get through but far fewer than have been anthologized. I was equally interested in what poets do: not intentions or ambitions but how they see themselves fitting in. And I was interested in poetry. Poetry has always been relevant, and maybe, looking back and despite what various critics say about readership or lack thereof, it has been central through the twentieth century and into the twenty-first in a way it had not been before. The university, for good and ill, was a safe space for poetry and its study. That is changing. Libraries rarely buy poetry books; there are fewer poetry-centric modules offered to undergraduates. English studies seems to be failing. People blame the academies or the academics—the modes of study—but that oversimplifies. The arts have been priced out, and poetry is the least monetary of the lot (*pace*, opera)—its creation does not require any overhead. People want comfort and reassurance; they want good jobs and happy endings. Poetry does not offer that. We are, as a species, as unrealistic as ever. And the place of poetry is changing. Right now, there is less of poetry as I have come to see it: fewer professional review bodies, less reading, less understanding.

The internet has offered an alternative to traditional publishing models, and it is here that almost everyone's energies are focused. All the way back in 1990, in a book that A.F. Moritz recommended to a younger me, Octavio Paz argued:

> I am certain that poems projected on the TV screen are destined to become a new poetic form. This genre will affect the dissemination and reception of poetry in a way no less profound than did, in its heyday, the printing press.
>
> (*The Other Voice*, translated by Helen Lane)

It never quite happened for television, but it is apparent on the internet that poetry will move in different directions. Poems are everywhere: cheap content for the content-hungry. No wonder that ChatGPT and its ilk can so easily emulate the arts. But there is little room for longer forms in this way: the epic—the song of the tribe—is not tweetable. Though various and silly critics argued that the fragment had gone its way in the twenty-first century, there is more fragmentation than ever, as the twentieth century revelled in it and offered little critique. Until poets can find ways to represent different forms, we will be trapped in the fragment and lyric of modernity.

There is, more often than not, an online lionizing of certain poets and not a celebration of poetry exactly. Some poetry books are selling, but that means publishers want more books like the saleable one. Where there was once variety, bookstores now stock fewer poetry books. It is not just in Canada. In Bavaria, where I spend a good amount of time each year visiting my in-laws, bookstores tend to have one row on a shelf for poetry—usually mixed in with "classics" from the seventeenth and eighteenth centuries. The selection is small: Rilke, Goethe, and sometimes a collection or two in translation—Elizabeth Bishop, Louise Glück (post-Nobel), and Ocean Vuong come to mind as recent sightings. I once saw a translation of Ashbery's *Flow Chart* in a bookstore in Augsburg. But that shop closed.

And yet poetry remains what it always was. Terror and tragedy, sometimes celebration: those are spaces where it remains a mainstay of our culture. The arrival of the medical humanities—art as a source of healing, poetry as purgative—is predictable. But anyone who feels better after writing a poem has not written a poem. Poetry is criticism and philosophy, both moralistic and barbaric, often at the same time. Why would anyone want that? Because for some of us, this kind of thinking—even the ability to think in this way—isn't just for sad occasions. It also means that we view the world differently.

With all this in mind, I wonder what a reader will make of these interviews. They began as critique and what is discussed is a Canada of the late-twentieth and early-twenty-first centuries that no longer exists. What is the Canadian tradition now in comparison to the nationalist mould that developed in the 1970s? Where is the centre of that tradition? I'm not certain.

What if one were to talk about a poetry of Canada, however, from the beginning and to where it might lead, that goes further back than Confederation—masterworks from Haida Gwaii, Persia, Ancient Greece, India, China, why not? Not limiting ourselves to anglo- or francophone traditions, all the ones that existed here and are brought to Canada could be welcome. Works in translation, yes, from all the traditions that exist in Canada simultaneously. A "language poetry" built of languages. What if Canada does not need a new centre but requires something more central to understanding what makes Canada? I will not offer any grand conclusions, but I do believe the interviews here point in that direction.

In preparing this book, I have made very few edits to the interviews. They remain mostly what they were. I have tried to update in some way the short biographical notes that begin each interview. Four of the poets are no longer with us. That is startling to me, a disheartening occasion. My aim was to keep the biographical notes then-contemporary, so that the publications we discussed and which I read are apparent, but nonetheless I did add more recent and sometimes posthumous publications. I have followed the work of these writers and can say I continue to admire them all.

The book ends with an interview with a non-Canadian, Michael Schmidt. The anthology that I co-edited and that Schmidt published in the UK began as a response to his flippant dismissal of the idea of Canadian poetry as "short street" in his book *Lives of the Poets* (1998). Details of that criticism are at the beginning of the interview, so I will not say too much more here. But Schmidt was not the first to make claims like this. We can go back to T.S. Eliot, who wrote in 1936, "I do not know of a single poet of the slightest merit in Canada, Australia and New Zealand."

Surprise! The outsider has a different perspective. I hope the inclusion of this interview will remind readers of the wider world of poetry and prevent writers from falling back into old garrison patterns. Larger, transnational perspectives allow a poet the freedom to explore more widely and more variously.

If I can impart one final message here—beyond the usual declarative to read poetry and buy poetry books—it is to listen to poets. The real ones among us offer a wisdom and a perspective at odds with prevalent visions. I read poems and tried to listen here to a good many poets of wisdom. That so many responded is a blessing. But there were others I did wish to hear from. Sometimes interviews began and never found their way. There is a file on my desktop, incomplete, a conversation with Eric Ormsby that life and work and two small children interrupted. And there is this, an email I had from Jay Macpherson, dated March 13, 2012, after I had written asking if she would let me interview her: "Unfortunately your request comes too late—I am in a palliative care home with probably a few days to go." She died on March 21.

Evan Jones
April 2023

Solitary Vice and Verse

DARYL HINE

Daryl Hine was born in 1936 in British Columbia. He studied classics and philosophy at McGill University and, after an interval abroad, earned a PhD in comparative literature at the University of Chicago in 1967. He taught at the University of Chicago, the University of Illinois, and Northwestern University. From 1968 to 1978, he edited *Poetry.* He then published six collections, including *Selected Poems* (1980), and two book-length poems, *Academic Festival Overtures* (1985) and *In & Out* (1989), both detailing events of his youth. In 1986, he was elected a MacArthur Fellow, receiving the prestigious "genius grant" for his work as poet and translator. Among his publications as translator of Greek and Latin were versions of *Ovid's Heroines* (1991), the erotic epigrams of the *Greek Anthology* in *Puerilities* (2001), and *Works of Hesiod and the Homeric Hymns* (2005)—for the latter, he was awarded the Harold Morton Landon Translation Award by the Academy of American Poets. *Recollected Poems: 1951–2004* appeared in 2007, *&: A Serial Poem* in 2010, and *A Reliquary and Other Poems*, posthumously, in 2013. He died in August 2012. At the time of this interview—October 2006 to March 2007—Hine lived in Evanston, Illinois.

You express throughout *Academic Festival Overtures*, and in your introduction to *Recollected Poems*, the naturalness of your sexual predilection. Is your identity as a poet, or artist, as natural?

Perhaps because my sense of my sexuality and writing poetry began about the same time—the poetry in fact a bit earlier—at the age of puberty (I hesitate to assign a causal relation here), and because I was fortunate in the information and models I found in books, which provided at once a validation for my feelings and examples of what could be done with words, I tend to regard both as equally natural to me. I have noticed how metaphorical even my ordinary conversation is—and my thought. But if one can be homosexual without engaging in homosexual acts, one cannot be a poet without writing poems. The earliest poem in this collection is to a boy with whom I was in love for years, though we never had sexual relations (see *Academic Festivals*, passim), though I did publish a few inferior poems before that in Canadian magazines.

In your introduction to *Recollected Poems*, you describe your formalism as an "involuntary choice." Is this the same kind of naturalness?

I began by writing free verse, but my acquaintance with the history of English poetry soon convinced me what a newfangled aberration this was; nonetheless, there are a few examples in *RP*. I found myself increasingly comfortable with metred, if not always rhymed, poetry, which I began writing, in my teens, unconsciously as if by ear.

What's also interesting about your early development is the reliance on books for "information and models," as you suggest.

Books were always very important for me, long before I began to write; I could read early and was always getting in trouble for reading under my desk in school. It was literature that provided models for my early poetry, and I have always urged young poets to read before they try to write.

Let's talk a bit about the books that were important to you at this stage. You mention Proust and a certain Mr. W.H. in *AFO*. But you're known for translations of classical texts as well as your poetry. Were your leanings entirely European modernist in the early days?

In addition to the Europeans and Americans I read in my early teens (T.S. Eliot, Marianne Moore, Dylan Thomas, Hart Crane, James Joyce, and, strangely, Gertrude Stein), I was captivated by Arthur Waley's translations of Chinese poetry. Like most Canadians then, I began French at thirteen, but Latin not until fifteen. Virgil, specifically bits of the *Aeneid*, constituted my introduction to Latin poetry, the lyrical pleasures of which, along with Greek, I did not discover until later.

When did you leave British Columbia, and did you see that move as the end of your adolescence?

I left BC for McGill in 1954, at eighteen, and did not go back for a visit until 1966. My motive for accepting the McGill scholarship rather than one at UBC was to get as far away as possible, to find a different language and culture, and yes, I guess in retrospect, to put an end to adolescence—though I never really believed in such psychological categories, at least at the time. I'm not sure that I ever outlived adolescence—or childhood.

I asked about adolescence because it seems to be a subject you return to in your work, in *AFO* in particular but also in "An Adolescent," among other poems. What about that age/category attracts you as a writing subject?

As that was the period when I learned my craft, and formed some of the opinions that were to influence my life, I suppose it has a certain nostalgic, even romantic, appeal— which I am very happy to have outgrown. The events of *AFO* are seen in retrospect.

In *AFO*, you write: "I sensed a peculiar, intimate and vital / Solitary vice and verse." Do you see the creation of poetry as onanistic or monastic in the same sense?

Certainly I think solitude a practical prerequisite for any individual creation. Only once in very special circumstances did I even partially collaborate (the first poem of *RP*, with my lover, Sam Todes, a philosopher who had published a paper on shadows), and though I have been involved in the production of four or five plays, I didn't see such unavoidable compromise as truly creative. As to onanism, while I guess there is an element of that, sublimated, in any creation, I shouldn't overemphasize it in poems that are after all directed to an unknown reader.

Do you write to a single, idealized reader?

Sometimes I have, in those poems (mostly collected in the second section of *RP*) which envisage a specific "you," though even there I am aware of a broader potential readership. Otherwise, in what I could call third-person poems, the appeal is simply to "the reader"—I shouldn't bother with all the grammar, metre, and metaphor otherwise.

Do you mean that it is for this unknown "reader" that you keep to grammar, metre, and metaphor?

All I meant was that grammar is a means of communication and thus indicates the desire to communicate, as metre has been until very recently the medium of verse. I should think that anyone open at least to my formalism would enjoy my poetry?

Charles Simic has written that he believes poets are talking to God. Do you agree?

Simic's statement makes sense. These matters are difficult to explain, let alone resolve. In my new long poem "&," I write: "What all those poems that I wrote in code / Meant I only know I do not know, / Except they came gratuitous as manna." Does that help?

"If anyone cared to question my understanding, / I answered smartly that understanding was not / As important for poetic appreciation / As the educational establishment thought" (*AFO* 80). **Is this the same kind of thought?**

You remember *AFO* better than I do, as I have not reread it since publication. But yes, one's basic principles and prejudices seldom change in a lifetime. I did not, of course, mean that understanding played no role in the appreciation of poetry, but that the kind of prose paraphrase which we were taught in school was secondary to the total effect of the poem. It should be no surprise that one of my favourite poets in late adolescence was Mallarmé.

Do you appreciate a sense of mystery in a poem?

Often, yes, though it certainly is not the first quality I look for. I have written both cryptic poems ("Arrondissements") and very plain ones like "Stanzas in Memoriam," which I like equally. My early work was taxed with obscurity, but what was obvious to me might be obscure to others.

Auden talks about obscurity in relation to *The Orators*. Perhaps this is a good time to ask about his influence.

Auden was a pervasive but not exclusive influence, and he is seldom obscure, unless in *The Age of Anxiety*. His clarity later made him difficult to teach. I saw a certain amount of him in New York, and he expressed a flattering regard for my poems. The term "wilful obscurity" is often used, as if that were worse than the involuntary kind. It's not something that I have ever worried about much.

What was Auden like? Could you explain a bit more why you felt he was difficult to teach?

I met him in '62 but continued seeing him on my visits to New York; the last time was here in '71. He was, in a word, grumpy—tired and not at all happy, though he could still be sharp and funny. Perhaps it was my affinity with his work that made it difficult to teach, but I always found it so admirably obvious that it did not lend itself to explication.

What was Montreal like in the 1950s, when you arrived? And your meeting with other poets, like Louis Dudek?

Montreal in the '50s was perhaps seedier, mostly two-storey—but I've seen very little of it since. Compared to BC, it seemed cosmopolitan and cozy and of course colder. I received a chilly welcome from Dudek at first. He sneered at the stanzaic poem I showed him, and asked would I be writing the same in ten years. (I did, I've never changed.) I was similarly unimpressed by his pastiche of Pound, for whom I never cared. He seemed to have forgotten this when, two years later, he offered to publish my second book.

Leonard Cohen was another poet Dudek "discovered." Who else was around then? Was there anyone whose work you were taken with?

Not very, though I knew and liked Leonard. More than Dudek, I liked Irving Layton and thought him a better poet. Frank Scott I also liked personally, though the poetry didn't interest me much. Ditto with John Glassco. Miriam Waddington was very kind to me.

The events of your long poem *In & Out* (first published in 1975) occur around this time. You converted to Catholicism and spent time in a Benedictine monastery before dropping out of university. What was the attraction of Catholicism in particular?

I visited the monastery between my freshman and sophomore years but didn't drop out till the end of my senior year, '55 and '58 respectively. The reasons for my "conversion" I have never really been able to fathom, except insofar as I may have done in *In & Out*. The appeal wore very thin very quickly. I took the rules of Catholicism, as I understood them, literally and, since these seemed to condemn me to a life of chastity, sought out the traditional place for that. But I think there are deeper motives: I've always lived a quasi-monastic life. My time in that actual monastery was brief: three months, about half the time I spent in the church.

Did you write or work on poems while in the monastery?

No, or not much. This was, I think, the least productive period of my life. Something in the belief system, maybe in the effort of belief itself, seemed inimical to the free exercise of imagination.

There was no connection, then, between religiosity and poetry?

Initially I think there might have been. You must remember this was half a century ago, when one of the charms of the Roman church for me was its use of Latin. But this appeal soon evaporated. I found the intellectual climate of Catholicism stultifying.

Let's talk about your European travels, which yielded a travelogue, _Polish Subtitles_ (1962). How long were you abroad, and which countries did you travel to? Did you have any interaction with writers abroad?

I was abroad from 1958 to 1962, first in the UK (about a year) and then in Paris, with short excursions to Poland, Italy, and Spain. I met a few other writers in all these places but spent more time in Paris with painters—not deliberately. I spent some weeks in Mallorca and saw quite a lot of Robert Graves, for whose sixty-fifth birthday I wrote a masque. If you want to know more, there is my only prose novel, _The Prince of Darkness & Co_ (1961). I haven't read that since either.

This is the second time you've mentioned that you haven't read one of your books since it was published.

I am uncomfortable reading about myself; I suppose it's like overhearing gossip about oneself: something to do with a dichotomy between subject and object. I am always a subject—well, _the_ subject.

What did you make of Graves?

I have very mixed feelings about Graves (whose poetry I never much cared for). He could be very charming and amusing but also cranky and silly—see his *Greek Myths*. On the whole, he was nice enough to me, as long as I remembered my place, but as I was twenty-two...! My book, *TPOD&Co*, couldn't be published in the UK as possibly libellous—RG was notoriously litigious.

The young generation of poets when you were in the UK included people like Philip Larkin and Thom Gunn. Were you in contact with either of them?

Not while living there. I met Thom Gunn merely once, and it is I think significant that he spent most of his life in California. Larkin's insularity is one of the things I find unsympathetic. But I do like Geoffrey Hill.

What is it about Hill that you admire?

What I would have to call his objectivity (as opposed to subjectivity), with which I sympathize. In going over my poems, I was struck by how seldom I use the first-person singular. But I am not comfortable with discussing contemporaries, whom I generally refused to review. Auden once said to me, "Poetry is not a horse race."

Let's move to New York in 1962, where you first met Margaret Atwood. How did that meeting come about?

She looked me up, on the recommendation of a mutual Canadian friend. She was a graduate student at Harvard at the time. I saw a lot of her in Cambridge as my friend Sam was teaching at MIT then. She invited me to read in Montreal, when she had her first job there, and most importantly at UBC in '66—my first visit there in a dozen years. When we met, Peggy had published nothing, and her subsequent career, while it hardly surprised me, was astonishing.

Is it even correct to think of your work as Canadian?

Not really; I've never been self-consciously Canadian, as a writer at least. By default, perhaps. I have always considered Canada an intermediate department of Anglo-American literature.

How did you meet James Merrill?

JM I met in Paris in 1960 and followed his advice to come to New York a year or two later. He was my closest literary friend, though there were other poets I had more in common with perhaps. Our affinity was as much personal as poetic. Funny, generous, and affected, he enriched my life for more than three decades. I like some of his poems very much, and I believe he liked mine.

Why did you move to Chicago?

I moved here in 1963, the last place I'd expected to spend my life, but such is the vanity of human wishes. There was nothing deliberate about Chicago. I had not completed my BA at McGill, and after five years in the world, supported partly by Canada Council grants and partly by literary odd jobs (CBC, BBC, reading for publishers), I was persuaded to seek the comparative security of academic life and took up graduate studies at the University of Chicago, which was willing to overlook my undergraduate debacle. This was ironic as I never did become a full-time academic, though I have a PhD.

Perhaps this is a good opportunity to ask about the professor–poet relationship. What are your thoughts?

I have mixed feelings but, on the whole, do not regard it as a bad thing. Though I never took a creative writing course, and did both my undergraduate and graduate work in classics, I have had to teach writing from time to time and had a few gifted and likeable students. For a poet, there could be much worse ways of making a living. On the other hand, the system has resulted, with a few exceptions, in a bland standardization, such that most modern poetry increasingly resembles itself.

How did the position at *Poetry* come about?

I was offered the job out of the blue by the previous editor (Henry Rago, whom I did not know) during my first year teaching at UC, where he also taught. It had never occurred to me to want it, but I could not resist. This was in '68—I lasted ten years. I didn't think much of Rago or his magazine, frankly. I disregarded any advice he gave me; I never saw any point in doing anything unless I could do it my own way. At the time of Henry's death (in '69), I was acting editor and was soon confirmed as editor. Henry's retirement, like that of my successor, was forced, whereas mine was voluntary. To these two, the editorship of *Poetry* was the pinnacle of their lives, while it was not of mine.

The anti–Vietnam War issue you edited, published September 1970, was the first openly political statement an editor of the magazine made. What was the public reaction to it?

The anti-war issue elicited a mixed but largely positive reaction. It contradicted my own suspicion that "poetry makes nothing happen" but expressed my indignation at the time.

Perhaps your example is that poets themselves make things happen?

If I don't really think that poetry can make much happen, despite the fact that the Vietnamese war ended not long after that issue of *Poetry*, I certainly don't believe that poets could or should have any extra-poetic influence on affairs. Not the poets I have known. Two poets who definitely made a difference were Luther and Mao Tse Tung.

Did you feel you were taking a risk at the time?

I suppose I was taking a risk, given the politics of the *Poetry* board, one of whom suggested I publish a pro-war issue, to balance, but I gave it little thought. I knew I was right, and history has amply confirmed that opinion.

You mentioned you voluntarily left the editorship at *Poetry*.

I may have been the only editor of *Poetry* to resign voluntarily. After ten years, I had had enough of what I found an increasingly sterile and unrewarding job and wished to return to academia.

It's been, if I'm not mistaken, fifteen years since your last book of poetry was published, but in that time, you've published three compendious translations of major Greco-Roman texts.

Though I wrote fewer poems in this period, some are among my best. I had always supplemented with translation, but the proportion has altered in recent years. I have to do something in the morning!

How does translating differ from writing your own poetry? Is there a difference between translator of poetry and poet?

At its best, there is no difference; the translator becomes the poet, and it is this for which he continually strives. Otherwise, it is a way of writing poetry without the need for a subject, which is supplied by the text, leaving the really interesting work to the translator.

One last question: Is it less difficult or more to translate a well-known text, like the *Homeric Hymns*?

Neither. I never read other translations and chose my texts on the basis of affinity with an author, such as Ovid or Theocritus, for instance. Oddly, I felt great affection for the *Homeric Hymns*, but none for Hesiod, which was commissioned. As to the nature of this affinity, it is inexplicable, like personal attraction—unless it be that I should like to write like that.

Thought's Backwaters

NORM SIBUM

Norm Sibum was born in Oberammergau, Germany, in 1947, grew up in Alaska, Missouri, Utah, and Washington, and moved to Vancouver in 1968. He has published poetry with presses in the UK and Canada, the most recent of which, at the time of the interview, were *The Pangborn Defence* (2008) and *Smoke and Lilacs* (2009). He has since published two further collections—*Sub Divo* (2012) and *Gardens of the Interregnum* (2020)—and a novel, *The Traymore Rooms* (2013). His *Girls and Handsome Dogs* (2002) won the Quebec Writer's Federation A.M. Klein Award for Poetry. This interview was conducted between November 26, 2008, and January 20, 2009. Sibum lives in Montreal.

You're the least biographical of poets, so perhaps we could start with some biography. You were born in Germany?

My descent is one of those complicated wartime stories, but both my parents were German-born, my father a peassant, my mother bourgeoise Berlin. I don't write about it because it's been done to death by scads of writers. Although I'm nearly as much European as I am an American (plus being a Caknucklehead as well), I don't feel that comfortable in Europe until I get over the Alps and into Italy. For the sake of protective camouflage, I have gone through life posing as a barbarian. It has been one of my more realized fantasies, sweeping into Rome on the train as a Visigoth.

I was wondering, if it's not too personal, about your decision to come to Canada.

Vietnam. It was everything it was advertised to be: horrendous. Those people who think it's all now water under the bridge are deluded. What divides keeps dividing forever. But my memory is somewhat fogged on the particulars. The impulse had seemed somewhat spontaneous, but actually, I do remember that I talked it out loud quite a bit with a group of Unitarians who ran a coffee house at that time in Olympia, Washington. One night, my father showed up in this den of iniquity, and to put it briefly, he indicated that if I was going to go, then go, I had his blessing in the matter. My father had been a lifer in the army. In effect, what he had to say trumped anti-war politics inasmuch as he had no great respect for officers who might get me killed for no good reason. The Unitarians had come out from Boston, were students of Roethke and readers of William Carlos Williams, a pretty eclectic crowd. Perhaps some of their eclecticism rubbed off on me, and which is why, some years later, the Black Mountain poetry world began to seem rather confining.

When did you move to Montreal? Do you see yourself as part of the Canadian literary history of that city?

Do I feel myself part of the literary history of Montreal? When I first read your question, I thought you meant Canada overall, and the answer would be that no, I don't feel a part of it. To the extent I'm uninterested in Canadian identity and in the various poetic quarrels—that is, west coast poetry versus east coast, which, in a very general sense, was (and I guess still is) an argument as to the virtue of a more freely practised poetic craft as opposed to the more formalistic. Et cetera. What I found when I first began meeting poets in Montreal was, so it seemed, a more independent-minded sort of poet. Poets who were and are more skeptical of things and leery of belonging to schools or even to a scene. This suited me fine. And for the first time in Canada, I felt no need to have to explain myself or in any sense apologize for what I write. In other words, a poem was good or bad on merits that hadn't much to do with prevailing fashions of thought and poetics. Coming to Montreal did me a great deal of good. There's almost something of a city-state atmosphere here, and although

I can't make its history my own as a Quebecker might in either official language, I feel much less of an outsider in this city than was the case in Vancouver, where, paradoxically enough, I had more trouble with the American expatriates than I had with the BCers. Exile is too fancy and culturally loaded a word now to describe what my condition has been, but the word does apply to me to some degree. One is both much less exiled than one assumes and is exiled from a great deal more than one realizes. Otherwise, I have kept pretty much to myself.

What you describe about Montreal seems to me to be the history of the better poets in that city. There's a quote by Irving Layton, for instance, about A.M. Klein as the great outsider—outside the French community because he was English, outside the literary community because he was a cosmopolitan sort of poet, and outside the Jewish community for the same reason. Is there a lineage there that might better suit your identity within Canada?

As I have read very little of Layton and Klein, I can't say I've taken anything from them which might expand my own practice of verse and add to the way I accommodate myself to this city. Perhaps there was a reason I came to Montreal, if one subscribes to the theory that nothing happens by accident. On the other hand, I'm sure it's purely coincidence, and if I look around and note that this was Layton's town and Klein's, and so forth and so on, well, so much the better, and it's not just an Anglo provenance. How about Robert Melançon, for instance?

This man, if anything, is doubly a maverick, writing in French as a Quebecker but availing himself of the entirety of the French and English traditions, not to mention the classical canon. I believe he's one of the most important poets on the continent, and no one knows, because of all the bloody walls. What has come to sustain me, after the time spent with Yeats, Eliot, Pound, et al., is my reading of the Roman poets. I have never really understood why they should sustain me, but I think it has something to do with distance, that the poetry is both so far away in time and yet so immediate. I'm pretty much a recluse, and they are such social poets. Go figure. Even so, when you would speak of "lineage," this is the lineage I have in mind as would bear on my own identity.

Why the Romans?

I have no idea. One is almost tempted to believe in the transmigration of souls. I won't settle for the cliché of reading the past in order to comprehend the present. I don't claim any success in the matter, just that to make something solid of those shadowy figures in ancient Rome satisfies me in some peculiar way; something compels me in this, and I really don't know why it's happening. I don't do it so as to make political statements, though I suppose one could, and it's been done. I am not even that interested in writing set pieces, though I have a few of those in my books, the latest being in *Smoke and Lilacs*. Perhaps the attempt, in the end, whatever the result, simply allows me to see waitresses and cabbies and cashiers in a somewhat sharper or at least different kind of relief—but I can't say. Or perhaps it's a way of giving the mundanities a slip for a brief time, and playing a kind of joke on my own particular stretch of time, and the waitress or the cabbie or the cashier just happen to stand on ground richer than the floor of Walmart.

Do you see the Romans as more pertinent now?

I have certainly had conversations with academics in which I was warned off the America–Rome analogue, and that the analogue was, if nothing else, old hat, a cliché, but in at least a couple of instances, it seems to me there are uncanny similarities, chief of which is the amount of power both ends of the analogue enjoyed, and enjoy, to do good and to do—and we may as well be blunt about it— evil. Another similarity is the religiosity of the Romans and the Americans, for better or worse. It certainly seems to me I have been watching America as "republic" drift into what has been called Caesarism, a condition which is not strictly fascistic but does have fascist tendencies. The state of mind of the early Christians fascinates me for what they may have or may have not been thinking in their daily routines on the Roman streets, how much was worship of the Christ figure, how much was taken up with simply trying to remain a human being in a mean reality. That the Roman world was a cruel world, there is no question. But so is the American world, despite its suburban comforts. Technological advances et al. It's such a huge subject, particularly in the way it has become personal with me. I was just downstairs in my local, drinking coffee, watching the snow fall, and it hit me that, when I first read Livy, for instance, and putting aside questions of the actual worth of the histories he wrote, it was, like sex is sometimes, a way of stopping time, cheating death. And what's more personal than that?

Can you tell me about your friendship with Marius Kociejowski?

I was introduced to Marius Kociejowski in London by a mutual friend. We eyed one another warily, a couple of roosters. I had already read Marius's essay, the one entitled "The Machine Minders," which was his commentary on the state of contemporary culture back in the '80s. He has long since disavowed it as immature, but even so, the effect of having read it has always stayed with me, and it remains for me a kind of signpost for when I find myself in confusion. In other words, I think machine minders and I am reminded of what art and culture have been for too long and are even now; it's bad enough they are not much more than disposable commodities subject to market forces; they are pills one pops, and eureka, one is cutting edge, comforted and consoled by the proximity of the glassy-eyed. It was Marius who brought my work to the notice of Michael Schmidt. Over the years, we have harassed and insulted one another; ours is, despite it all, something like an affectionate relationship. He has a horror of the casual in poetry; I am pretty much the barbarian he can't quite remove from the landscape.

Even so, my love of the poetry and writings of Leopardi, for instance, is as deep as his; and after Leopardi, all the radical chic of a Warhol is pretty damn insipid stuff. A respite from the stuffily academic on all fronts turned into the endless vacation from hell. Well, I'm speaking in generalities here, but I think you get my drift.

That's the second time you've said "barbarian" in reference to yourself.

Now, barbarian poet. Actually, it's sort of a running joke between myself and Kociejowski, as he thinks me very uncouth, if not uncivilized. But there's a monster in me whom I dub Herr Professor, and one way of mitigating the damage he can possibly wreak is to think of myself as a barbarian. Also, as I mentioned, the very first time I entered Rome by train (overnight from Vienna), I had just the barest glimpse of how a barbarian might have felt, coming across the ancient city for the first time, and it's how I saw it—with awe.

A number of the poems in *The Pangborn Defence* are addressed to characters—Lunar, Crow, and Meredith Owens—and in "Answering Crow," you write:

> What's so much more to the point than an alias,
> Monicker, epithet, term of endearment, nexus
> For all that's good and brave and true in the face
> Of all that's wrong, than our voices pitched low among
> The zinnias and lilies, peonies, marigolds,

> Are the shadows now creeping into the realm
> From a place where the sun has no purchase.

Meredith Owens was an Islamicist who died in 1966, but his life and relationship to you in the poem remind me of the poet and scholar Eric Ormsby. Can you tell me more about Crow and Lunar? Is Marius Kociejowski Lunar?

Well, I shouldn't go and blow anyone's cover. But there is a quite-hilarious story as to how the nickname, alias, sobriquet Lunar came about in the first place, and it has nothing to do with any doing of mine or Lunar. I merely pounced on it with something akin to glee. As for "Crow," the crow is Crow's favourite bird, for all that this sentence is an echo chamber. And the thing about Crow is that, though he's a French Quebecker, and it took me a while to realize what follows here, that he's the most profoundly American of North Americans in the best sense of Jeffersonian, the "enlightenment" and all that, and, I suspect, he's the last of a certain mentality that refuses to indulge what's glibly and fatuously oracular, and I argue with him all the time, and he pities me. Ormsby? His best poems are always greater than the sum of their parts, and when I scratch my head and wonder how he does it, it's as if I encounter strata of Hart Crane, Edgar Allan Poe, Frank O'Hara, E.A. Robinson, not to mention Rexroth, say, or Robinson Jefferson in the work, and so forth and so on. I've seen his work dismissed by the silliest of criticisms rendered by the silliest of critics who couldn't find their collective tush if you gave them a helping hand, and if this is as good as it gets, I don't hold out much hope for the future of literature, and poetry in particular, in this neck of the woods.

In your poems, there's an everydayness of grocers and waitresses, and then there's the classical world between that and the poet. These two things are locked together while expressing a sort of alienation ("And truly, I inhabit thought's backwaters..."). This alienation is not necessarily linked to either the urban or the classical—it's not condescension in any sense—but is it an irony separating poet from subject matter?

I don't know that I have ever felt alienated as such, at least not in the sense the word has come to us through, for instance, certain writings. (I have Sartre in mind whose writings I mistrust, but then it's been years since I've read the man.) But I have to say that in the past few years, especially as the regime of G.W.B. has worn on, I have certainly felt something akin to alienation and something other than just disgust. I am not a scholar, but I have, at times, experienced the curious sensation of an elaborate set of mirrors when I muck about in Tacitus or Livy, or in any other aspect of the canon, or as when I hear out some speech on the senate floor broadcast on the media; in other words, I can see the US in the classical histories, and I can hear Tacitus in the rhetoric of certain American senators; I'm thinking of the speech Robert Byrd gave at the outset of the Iraq war. I could provide more examples, but I think what I'm saying here is concrete enough. Now I don't get this sensation when I read Napoleonic history, say, or when

I read about the Mayans or the Incas or even, necessarily, Periclean Athens.

What do you see as the role of the poet in the twenty-first century?

A poet's only obligation is to write the best poetry he or she can, and the rest follows. Otherwise we get bad poetry sanctified by some "cause" or another. More excuses to write badly. Poets have always been rather marginal to any society in which they function, the Greeks of a certain era perhaps the famous exception. Druidic poets had a high profile. Roman poets were pretty much non-entities in their day, though they might have the ear now and then (Virgil, Horace) of Caesar, some Maecenas paying the bills, picking up the bar tab. This "Roman" business is quite personal with me, and a lot of it stems from the fact that Rome in the beginning was a cow town, and a rather wild one at that, and I've certainly known the odd cow town or two. And the fact that Livy, in writing about Numa, could not comprehend the Latin of Numa's priestly mumbo-jumbo—well, for some reason or another, this really struck me, and the day is coming when the Gettysburg Address is going to suffer the same fate.

How does one of your poems take shape?

For the most part, I go through endless revisions of a poem. Usually, it has to do with hitting the right tone, getting it to sound right in my ear, apart from other considerations of form. I imagine myself standing in a room full of people: blind drunk. If, in this condition, I were to stumble somewhere in the reading of the poem aloud, then something's wrong with it, the lines, for some reason, not flowing properly. In other words, the poem should deliver itself, as it were, the poet incidental to the process. And I tend to write long poems, and I'm well aware that long poems go very hard on an audience, let alone readers of the page. And just as often it has to do with content, the reasons for all those revisions. What in hell am I on about now and why? Does anyone need this? The fact that I might need it—well, is it justification for a poem's public existence as opposed to the purely private one? Occasionally, certainly not very often, a poem comes to me whole and seems only to need a bit of tinkering. I'm very dubious of poems that come easily. What easy lies might I be telling? What gibberish tricked up as eloquence? Et cetera. And yet, for all the revisions, anything remotely resembling the barest hint of a work completed remains woefully unattainable, and it all seems so futile. Maddening. I figure poets are masochists, at least the good ones. Their opposites? Well, the answer as to what they are almost supplies itself. No need to pile on.

What about that audience? Do you have an ideal reader in mind when you write? Do the cabbies, grocers, and waitresses fit into your vision of a readership? I take the image of you drunk at a reading as example, but is there something more metaphorical there in the performative aspect? A persona? A vision of the poet? Perhaps there's that alienation again?

God help us from any more "vision of the poet," persona, role, ideal, or otherwise. I'd rather watch clowns performing in the street, only that too seems to have become chic. And besides, poetry is not an elective course; it's more like a curse one has incurred somehow. The only thing worse than making poetry is not making it. The muse is not a very sympathetic figure. I have no ideal reader as such in my mind when I write, but there are certain people I would hope to please, and there are certain people I would delight in displeasing. Most of the time, I have a conversation ongoing in my mind with either real persons or even imaginary interlocutors. I think all this is fairly standard, nothing new in it. What's a poem, anyway, but a suggestion even when pitched in an expressly declarative mode? Poems about one's feelings are despicable, but poetry without passion isn't going to go very far. If there's one thing that always drives me around the bend, it's this notion that poetry is somehow self-expression and so subversive because empowering. Bollocks. If one flatters oneself that one is being subversive, one has already been taken prisoner. Poetry is of the moment, without qualifiers and special appeals, and yet it's of all time and for all time and for keeps. If there's anything like ideal poetry, which I doubt, this then would be that ideal.

Could you elaborate a bit on the poem as suggestion?

The least apologetic poems of which I know—*The Iliad*, for example, or *The Divine Comedy*—don't waste time with being "suggestive"; they declare this is how it is or how it was, take it or leave it. Yet for me, at least, poems are but suggestions at bottom, because poets are human beings, not gods. Perhaps, as Aristotle put it (or was it Plato or both?), poets enter some divine state and then bring back the goods to mortals, but even so, Homer or the Homers were human, not godly, and it's said that Dante was not a particularly nice person. What I'm trying to say is that no poet, because human, can see the entirety of human experience at any given time, let alone understand in full the operations of the universe; yet a poet might get, as here I'll cheekily submit, a sniff; and then said poet may spend a lifetime attempting to explicate of what that sniff consists. Sex, death, and taxes, anyone? I think Shakespeare is perhaps beloved because he doesn't expunge doubt from his poetry, his own or that of his characters, and yet he's as clear-eyed as either Homer or Dante for all that his humanity shows. I suppose that the world in which Homer wrote had no room for Prufrocks—such neuroticism would get them killed in an instant—but Homer had to please his lords and masters, and what they wanted was the poetry of the warrior, with all their relentless terribleness plus the quirks, and Homer delivered it, but without romanticism. He's the least sentimental and most grim of poets, minus all that Wagnerian hullabaloo of Siegfried and so forth. But was Homer's so-called vision the only reality of eighth century BC, let alone the late Bronze Age? Perhaps Hesiod is the poet to read for that. And perhaps I haven't really addressed your question, but when a poet can be sure about something, he should be sure; as for the rest of it, a little honesty might gain him a reader's trust.

There's a pessimistic tone in your two most recent books, which I think you've suggested here is a sign of the times. Will the incoming presidency offer any reprieve?

Off the cuff, I would answer that there's a sense of futility with things and that, notwithstanding a million good intentions, things won't get better until we bottom out, as it were, and all the chaos in our minds drifts away. It's the sense that things have really gotten out of control, if they were ever under control, and of watching worlds smash apart into pieces and wondering what will take their place and not liking very much what appears to be taking shape. And yet, there's reason to feel hopeful and to dismiss one's pessimism, the inaugural on telly now. But then, one can't really know anything, predicting the future's a mug's game. My question is, one just jotted down in the journal I keep: How long before a new world begins to reach back for the history it succeeded? Before those shadows reassert? In any case, yes, a reprieve. The new tone was set. The rebuke, however veiled, was delivered. It does the soul good to hear it.

Where Then My Verses?

Marius Kociejowski was born in 1949, on a farm near
Bishop Mills, Ontario. In 1973, he left Canada and settled
in London after a year of travelling. His first collection of
poetry was *Coast*, published in 1991, followed by *Doctor
Honoris Causa* (1993) and *Music's Bride* (1999). A Canadian
edition of his poems, which collected the above, *So Dance
the Lords of Language*, was published in 2003. He has also
published two books on Syria, *The Street Philosopher and
the Holy Fool: A Syrian Journey* (2004) and a sequel, *The
Pigeon Wars of Damascus* (2010), and edited the anthology
Syria through Writers' Eyes (2006). He lives in London
and has published several books since this interview and,
at the time, was at work on a record of a world journey
through London's exile and émigré artists, writers, poets,
and musicians, published in 2014 as *God's Zoo: Artists,
Exiles, Londoners*. His most recent books are *A Factotum
in the Booktrade: A Memoir* (2022) and *The Serpent Coiled
in Naples* (2022). This exchange was conducted between
October 28 and December 2, 2010.

Would you mind telling me a bit about your background?

I grew up in the middle of nowhere, on a farm near Bishops Mills, Ontario, a small village which nobody has ever been to and which very few people left. My father was Polish, my mother is English, which probably accounts for my European as opposed to Canadian frame of mind. (Mind you, people of similar background often become more Canadian than the Canadians.) My parents had no aptitude for farming whatsoever and made the fatal mistake of naming their cows. After failing miserably in high school—not, I like to think, because I was stupid but because I couldn't have cared less, I then went to Ottawa, spending several years there, going to college and then to university, before leaving Canada forever in 1973. We settled in England after almost a year of travelling through the continent and with an extended stay of three months in an oasis town in Tunisia, which we chose because it had nothing whatsoever to entice the tourist. It was there that I was first smitten by the Arab world, although this did not find any resolution until 1995, when I went to Syria.

Can I ask, about Canada, did you plan to leave forever?

I wish I could say yes, because it would serve to feed that bit of me that wants to mythologize my past. The simple truth is I did not plan to stay in Europe nor did I plan to return to Canada. At the same time, I think I knew I had come to a dead end. I was in a new relationship with the woman who would become my wife. She had a sense of decorum, and I had been living as a slum dweller with a dog that crapped everywhere. I slept on a mattress on the floor of this dingy little apartment above a fish warehouse. It got so I no longer noticed the smell. There were no sheets on the bed, only army blankets. You might say I was going nowhere. I already had my moment of triumph in Ottawa, a week reading with the jazz group Weather Report, and I ran a poetry-reading series. I was a local face. Anyway, it was time to put on a clean shirt. A publisher in Toronto expressed an interest in publishing a collection of my poems, but I never responded. Had I done so, it might well have altered the course of my life. I might have stayed and written badly enough to be comfortable there. I simply quit a scene that had long ceased to feed me. A couple of years later, in a new country, knowing I had to start over from scratch, I destroyed all that work. The strange thing is I have a recurring dream about going back to Ottawa and going into a bookshop where I climb a ladder to a high shelf from which I pull a volume in plain black cloth and which I open to discover all those poems. The title of the book is *The Ottawa Poems*, and I cringe to see them. I thought they had been destroyed.

How do you see the UK poetry scene differing from the Canadian one you left behind?

Show me a poetry scene and I will set loose my torpedoes on it. Any poetry scene is to be avoided like the plague, and it amazes to observe how so many poets would do almost anything to enter that most contaminated of zones. If you were to ask me what my view of the scene in the UK is, I'd say it's smug and self-satisfied, although not at the nadir it was a few years ago with the "New Gen" nonsense. That really was repulsive. With respect to what is happening in Canada at present, I will have to remove myself from any further discourse. I can speak of a few individuals—Norm Sibum and Eric Ormsby, for example, although both of them are Americans!—otherwise, I have not followed what's happening over there. Actually, I have lost track of what's happening *here*. When I think back to Canada in the '60s and early '70s, it was in the grip of nationalist fervour, with endless discussions as to what constitutes a Canadian identity. There is no quicker way to destroy an identity than to put it on the dissection table. You had, on one hand, Margaret Atwood with the blighted knowledge of her literary tract, *Survival*, of which *Surfacing* was the fictional equivalent, both of them turgid in the extreme, and on the other, you had the informed ignorance of Al Purdy. I remember reading a poem he wrote about Hiroshima, this after he had been awarded Arts Council money to go there, at the end of which he shrugs his shoulders with a "Huh, what do I know?" response and talks about bringing in the groceries. This struck me as not only obscene but militantly stupid. That was the Canadian "poetry scene." I think it has probably smartened up a little. At that stage, I was already looking to other horizons, finding on them poets who would rise to form the constellation by which I might take my bearings. I had just discovered Zbigniew Herbert, and it was at that point I began to feel, as I still do, that I was some kind of European poet stranded in the English language.

When I think of the poets who have mattered most to me in this country—W.S. Graham, Geoffrey Hill, and, absentee though he is, Christopher Middleton—they are not of any scene. English poets have always been at their best when they are lone wolves. Put them in a literary cage and they begin to perform unnatural acts.

You left Canada almost forty years ago, but the epithet Canadian has stayed with you all these years (Michael Schmidt, for instance, has identified you as such in *Lives of the Poets*). Are you Canadian?

I always feel faintly embarrassed to be described so, and when he least expects it, I shall be taking extreme measures against Michael Schmidt. I have no desire to be rude about those who were my countrymen once, and there is, of course, a trend among Canadians abroad to be "in denial." It is not a position I wish to adopt. If I may be absolutely truthful about this, I have never felt Canadian. This is largely a matter of circumstances. I grew up in the heart of rural Protestant Ontario, at a period in its history when it was extremely difficult for people such as my parents who were nominally Catholic and very much from outside. Their first years were marked by extreme poverty, but no material poverty is as great as that of mental isolation. There was nobody with whom my father could discuss history, especially his own tragic one, and with my mother it was probably even more difficult in some ways, in that she shared a language bound by mutual incomprehension. In that situation, you either become more Canadian than the Canadians themselves or you retreat even deeper into yourself.

So for you, as traveller, there is no *nostos*?

It was not until I was in my mid-forties that I began to think more deeply on the matter of what it is to write about *place*. It was a question I had to ask myself, and my conclusion was that I travel not so much through physical scenes as I do through people. The *nostos* of which you speak was, or rather came to be, one of my poetic themes. I maddened myself almost, spending nine years on a poem of only forty-eight lines, entitled "Coast," which probably is a failure. I'll stand by it all the same. It draws not just on Captain Ahab dashing against the deck "his heavenly quadrant" and choosing instead the "mere dead reckoning of the error-abounding log"—the passage in which Melville is at his most prophetic, maybe accidentally so—but also I had in mind the Odysseus theme. The difference is that, for the speaker in my poem, which may or may not be me, "there is no way home." There can be no touching the coast of home. "So shall we make darkness our corridor" is the poem's discomforting conclusion. Mind you, I blossom in the dark. It must be my Polish blood.

This brings us nicely to your first book of poems. I was thinking of your poem "The Return," where you write, "I surrender to a city / Buried beneath a city." In the poem, the poet seems to me both Oedipus and Hermes, blind exile and god of travellers in one: "My feet had sight, /

My feet were winged / But are now made blind." There's a definite sense of the wounding of the return.

Oedipus and Hermes were not in my mental landscape, but now that you have put them there, they seem to fit and I am happy enough to put on the kettle for them. I think one does, on occasion, stray out of one's time, and if there is any pain in this poem, it is not in the arrival, surely, but in the departure. "A bracelet slips down / the length of a raised arm": I feel sure I have seen that woman somewhere.

To continue the Homeric reading of this poem, is the woman Nausicaä or Penelope? That is, is this the final return or only a return to a familiar place, people, and language?

Well, if I *had* to choose, it would be the former, the "burner of ships," but in truth, she is just some sensual creature I might have spotted in an ancient marketplace. The return is to somewhere I'd never been before, which, I think, is allowable in verse. The imagination is, after all, promiscuous, is it not?

Imaginative promiscuousness: is that a good way to think of the manner in which you begin a poem?

I don't believe there is a good way to think about beginning a poem. If there were, if one could locate that door which, once opened, allows the Muse admittance, then maybe one might be able to write poems forever. There is no manner.

There are, on the other hand, conditions that allow for poetry, and in this respect, I'd say the mind going wherever it wishes, or attaching itself to whatever it likes, can result in the occasional surprise, when the lines seem almost to write themselves. I can remember times when this has happened to me. This is not a recipe, of course, for rambling, or, worse still, self-expression, because the deeper surprises rarely come if one is not already in a state of some concentration. The rest is discipline.

Reading "Giacomo Leopardi in Naples" this morning, I came across, in the second verse paragraph, which ends, "Should they win, where then my verses?", a sense of who is not your reader. It's the reader with faith you're interested in. Can you tell me more about that faith? About that kind of reader?

Some punk in Canada, a critic, suggested that I had composed my Leopardi poem by drawing on material I had gathered on the internet. The poem was written before I ever knew how to switch on a computer, and in fact it is, despite the literary persona, based on a wealth of personal experience. The line you quote came from a memory of a group of yuppies in a wine bar at the height of the Thatcher years—graduates from the disco floor to the City, brash and empty, just the sort of people she admired—but I do not wish to wag a finger at the semi-literate. Incidentally, the line has impact only if you consider the preceding two: "They drape the skeleton of all things with their festering pride, / And fearing the tumble through endless space wage war upon silence." If they win that war, then we really will be in serious trouble. Actually, we already are. I will go further and say the people most harmful to the continuance of literature are writers themselves. They are self-professed "readers." So where does faith come into this? As soon as one tries to define faith, one risks mawkishness, but perhaps you will permit me to come at this from another angle. When I realized, at the age of nineteen or so, that I would become a writer, it was, in a sense, a decision to undertake a pilgrimage, a secular one to be sure, but one that would mean sticking to the line of my life, no matter what. I was not unique in this. This was the position of most artists at that time. There was, if you like, certain holiness to being a poet. One might go to hell with it, fuel the flames with sex and drugs and alcohol, but at least one did so without compromise or with recognition of what needed to be preserved. What we have witnessed in the past forty years is wholesale degradation in all the arts, and I think the moment things went bad was when art ceased to be a vocation and became a profession. And as soon as it did, poets became performers, and as soon as they became performers, they began to serve the twin gods of celebrity and entertainment. That this should have happened at all is bad enough, but their attitude has been supported to the hilt by government-aided bodies. It has become so you can tell that crowd in the wine bar that X is a genius—all you have to do is say so ten times in a row—for example, "Damien Hirst is a genius, Damien Hirst is a genius…" (ten times)—and although they may know not of what they speak, they will be reading X's works or hanging it on their walls or dancing to its tune. You even have poets being paid to make fools of themselves by taking poetry into the corporate world—or to Wimbledon, for God's sake. It would be preferable if they took their poetry to the latrine. They may find themselves there. I need hardly tell you where their faith has gone. It went up for sale. I don't even need to say what it is. It's wherever you hear the clinking of coins. Rimbaud saw what was coming when he wrote about everything being for sale. I am not wholly without hope. I believe that culture is like a river and that, every so often, it goes underground and we have little idea where or when it will re-emerge, but it is down there somewhere, flowing still. One consequence of this, however, is that in the meantime, people are deprived of their ability to judge. They are nervous for fear of being wrong, and so they let the commissars of culture do the judging for them.

And what about your own faith?

I could, of course, say it is a private matter, but this too often seems a way of circumventing the issue. Also, it is a failure to address one's own silences. There is nothing that disturbs me more than atheism, especially the militant kind expounded by Hitchens and Dawkins, which seems to me rooted in the deepest kind of arrogance. I am deeply fearful of a godless universe. Scientific materialism is a form of hell worse than anything religious systems have produced. The aforementioned will say otherwise. Atheism seems to me a closing of the imaginative faculties, a denial of wonderment. When I listen to Bach,

I believe. But what kind of cultural god have I made for myself? What is this elite club to which I have been denied membership? Maybe it would be easier for me to say, yes, God exists, but I find myself not fully able to believe in Him. With faith, there can be no half measures. I find myself envious, and respectful, of other people's faith, and for a Dawkins to throw mud in their faces is utterly contemptible. I might argue that every atheist's currency is God. Where would they be without God? That argument fails, however. Atheism is so, so comfortable. I can't bear religiosity either—those pinched faces. I feel quite at home with those who genuinely, and humbly, believe. Agnosticism strikes me as the worst of all possible fates, a blind stumbling from empty room to empty room. I wish to be spared that, and yet maybe that's where I am, the tips of my fingers reaching out into nowhere. I'd much prefer to be one of John Donne's "honest doubters."

Reading over *So Dance the Lords of Language*, it seems to me you build yourself anew in each poem (even as you arrive at some similar themes, form is as varied as content). And in this interview, so far, as I try to connect your poems, you seem to sidestep the spotlight by returning me to particulars. Is that the connection in your poems—their various and varied fascinations in and of themselves?

I am guided by superstition or whim or a flickering in the nerves. All I know for sure is that every time I set out to write a poem, it's as if I'm doing so for the first time, which already sounds like the opening line of an awful song. Maybe it's because I've written so few poems that each of them presents a major challenge. What you say is most observant, though, in that, yes, I do tend to return people to particulars. I am much more interested in the connections between poetry and life than in any ideas concerning poetry. We all have our different sets of references, of course. I read the thirteenth-century *Journal* of Friar William of Rubruck, an account of his travels among the Tatars, and in it he describes how when the Tatars rode out—for rape and pillage, one supposes—they would never go back the road by which they came. They would always seek out an alternative route. That strikes me as a good guiding principle for one's artistic endeavours. Also, I have suspiciously high cheekbones, which may point to certain irregularities in my Polish ancestry.

Your own set of references are often, mostly, historical and, perhaps occasionally, obscure in their particulars. I think here of "Dinu Lipatti Plays Chopin's Sonata in B Minor," with its epigraphs from *The Tempest* and Sir Thomas Browne. Can you tell me a bit about connecting those sources to your poem?

Here again, as with so many of my poems, especially those that *appear* to be historical, this came out of personal experience. I wouldn't see the point of writing it otherwise. I am not interested in historical literary exercises. Dinu Lipatti will not be obscure to anyone with a love of classical music, but in truth, it matters little whether people have heard of him or not. The true subject of the poem is the woman who is not, as some have made her out to be, elderly but rather on the cusp of middle age. Actually, the woman on whom I based her was some years younger, but when it came to writing the poem, I "aged" her a little so that she would be the age she had become at the time of writing. I met her only the once. She had been a successful concert pianist in Budapest, but when she came to London in hope of furthering her career, she was unable to break into the musical scene. That night, she introduced me to the playing of Lipatti, and the mental image I preserve of her is of this woman, highly strung as Hungarians tend to be, kneeling on the floor, in front of one of those cheap portable record players from the '60s, and putting on a scratchy record. What was most touching about her, at that moment, was that the top buttons of her blouse were undone. This is not being lascivious. She was attractive, certainly, but so absorbed was she in the pianism of this great artist, she did not notice. Consequently, her sexuality was at a strange remove. The eroticism was in her response to the music. It must have been ten years or more before she entered my poem, unbidden. I can't remember precisely when I discovered the Thomas Browne quote, but it is a marvellous statement about music being reflective of the divine order. The Shakespeare quote is what it is. So, really, there is very little that is obscure in the poem. One always cheats a little, of course: when, in the poem, she describes her professor as "a man with a monkey's face," this was in fact an English professor I had once. She and I had nothing resembling that conversation.

So there's fiction to your recollection of personal experience in the poem?

Yes, but only insofar as it's true.

I ask because poets tend not to discuss the fiction side of their poems. Can you say a bit more?

I don't think poetry has a fiction side, which is what distinguishes it from the novel. And even there I need to be careful, because the very greatest novels, those which are poetically true, Dostoevsky and Cervantes, for instance, do not have a fiction side. A poem that *works* is true. It is a synthesis of elements that are real. It is for this reason that a poem is overly susceptible to exposure. It will not allow for the intrusion of the false. When, on occasion, the false does intrude, it is painfully evident, more so than in any other literary form. This is not to abolish the notion of invention, which is something else altogether. Milton's Satan is not a fiction but a magnificent invention. So, too, is Dante's *Commedia*.

Where does a poem like "Giacomo Leopardi in Naples" fit between invention and truth?

I have, of course, appropriated the figure of Leopardi for my own purposes. It is an awful gamble, an act bordering on the irresponsible, putting words into somebody else's mouth, but my hope is that his spirit will give me leave. With that poem in particular, it is full of things I have seen. It is also based on things I read about him. You asked me earlier about my poetics. Maybe I should mention the little note Goya made in the corner of one of his sketches for *The Disasters of War*: "*Yo lo vi*" ("I saw it"), which could serve as an artistic credo. Another is the two lines at the end of W.S. Graham's "Johann Joachim Quantz's Five Lessons": "Do not be sentimental or in your Art. / I will miss you. Do not expect applause." There is also what Solzhenitsyn wrote in *The Oak and the Calf* about how it takes imagination to see things as they are. So I would say that, in purely artistic terms, there is nothing between invention and truth.

What drew you to Syria in 1995?

I was in Cambridge having lunch with Christopher Middleton when he pulled from his pocket an ancient coin from Antioch. An avid collector of coins of the Roman Empire, he began to explain to me that the coin must have been minted by someone who was illiterate, because it had a misspelling on it. Christopher is one of the most seductive of people, because when he speaks of something and does so with enthusiasm, one cannot help but pursue the subject. I went to the library and took out a book on the history of Antioch and was beguiled by a single sentence describing how the streets of the city had been set at such an angle as to catch the breeze blowing off the Orontes. I knew I had to go there. A couple of months later, on a whim almost, I phoned up an airline to enquire whether they had any tickets to Damascus. There was a single seat available at a bargain price. I took it. I flew to Damascus, arriving there after midnight, without so much as a guidebook and without having booked a room in advance. It was the beginning of a journey of misadventure. Almost immediately, I fell in with low life. I was taken unawares to a brothel, got robbed, not there but elsewhere, I was bitten by some mysterious insect, a couple of hundred bites that took three months to clear up, and then, after skipping the clutches of the police, who wanted to keep me in situ until they caught the thief, who was, technically speaking, a New Yorker of Syrian descent, I got ill. I did not, by the way, reveal the identity of the thief, otherwise I would never have got out of there. I had so little money left, I was forced to cut my trip short, but such was the kindness of the Syrian people who helped me at every turn that I made a vow to return. The whole point of this story is that I never made it to Antioch. I had not realized Antioch was no longer in Syria but had been annexed by Turkey in 1939. The book I'd read was published some years before then.

You seem over and over again in your travel books uncomfortable with the notion of travel literature itself. Can you expand on this some? It seems to me the particulars you address are much like the particulars of your poetry.

I wonder if there is anyone out there who knows when the phrase "travel literature" first came into use. I bet it was some bookseller wondering where to shelve his stock. Clearly, it is quite recent and would seem to have been coined at a point when *travel* as we used to understand it, when it was a matter of entering unknown spaces, had ceased to be. I suspect the last true travel writer was Wilfred Thesiger. After all, there is nowhere on the globe one cannot get to with relative ease. Can one truthfully write anymore about going to a place? I think the onus on any writer now is to write from *out of a place*. With the very emergence of "travel literature," there has been a corruption of sorts. There is a breed of writer who self-dramatizes, and there is another who continually jokes, and yet another who grabs onto a gimmicky theme. This said, I think the genre is responsible for some of the best prose in the language. If you were to ask me which I prefer—a roomful of poets or a roomful of travel writers—it would always be the latter, if only because they are interested in things outside themselves. As to the particulars you mention, and I speak for myself only, I should like to think the distance between the concerns of poetry and prose is not that great, although, heaven forbid, I would hate to produce poetic prose. A poet's prose is something else.

You write of the desert "as being a place for both the sharpening of faith and language," bringing us back nicely to faith.

I am speaking of the Islamic faith, of course, although equally one could apply this to the early Christian desert wanderers. A Bedouin once, when I asked him if there were any poets in his tribe, explained to me that the desert and the stars and the silences made poets of all his people. Which of them did I wish to speak to? In early times, a poet would go into the desert in order to purify his language. I would say that, for the Muslim, faith and language are inextricable, the Quran being for him the highest and, of course, the purest form of Arabic.

Sulayman, in *The Street Philosopher and the Holy Fool*, asks, "Why do you write? Always there is renewal, even in your face and in your physical movements, in your behaviour, too. If you watch this continual process of renewal you will see God Himself, the true Allah." Is this you, Marius, pinned down by the holy fool?

Oho! Yes, maybe. If I may make a fine distinction: when speaking to the people about whom I write, although I may not believe what they believe, I believe they believe. It is not for me to question the integrity of their faith but to accept it for what it is. I seek to be invisible.

Bigtime Tennis

Don Coles was born in Woodstock, Ontario, in 1927. He studied history at the University of Toronto, finished a second degree in English literature at Cambridge in 1954, and subsequently lived in London, Stockholm, and Munich, initially on a grant, later as a translator. From 1965 to 1995, he taught humanities and creative writing at York University in Toronto; for ten of those years, he was also poetry editor for the May Studio at Banff. He published eleven books of poetry, including, in the UK, *Someone Has Stayed in Stockholm: New and Selected Poems* (1994); in Germany, *Die Weissen Körper der Engel* (translated by Margitt Lehbert, 2007); a book of translations from the Swedish of Tomas Tranströmer; a novel entitled *Doctor Bloom's Story* (2004); and a memoir, *A Dropped Glove in Regent Street* (2007). He died in November 2017. This interview was conducted between September 24 and November 4, 2011. Coles lived in Toronto.

I want to begin by asking about time in your poems, specifically in "Someone Has Stayed in Stockholm," which seems to me a speculative poem, describing in detail an alternate universe.

I don't think there's a single poem (mine or others'), among those I know best and re-read most often, that doesn't owe at least half of its core appeal to time. Whatever else is at play will lead towards a last line or last stanza or simply a gathering cumulative awareness that all the images, all the words, all the faces and places that initially, when first met, may have seemed almost randomly offered, may have seemed to have lived out their brief standalone existence and then to have fallen off the page—that all these are at poem's end now returned, they're rising up in my (and surely, I will then feel, every other reader's) mind as richly and as deeply and, because they have returned out of what seemed to be lost time, even more intensely than they can ever have been felt to be before.

It's a wonderful moment, or feeling, and one can be as grateful to whoever has put it before one's eyes as one can be for anything.

Right now, speaking as one who has been identified, in reviews, as a poet who's concerned with time, I may as well say that it's something I know needs to be there in anything I'm at work on. It will always be there, whether I go looking for it or not—that's obvious; but "looking for it" is likely to be good idea.

The poem "Someone Has Stayed in Stockholm," which, as you have suggested, could also be related to the idea of an "alternate universe," immerses itself in a place which is other than its author's usual habitat (although in this case, it's a place I did, for a few years, inhabit), an immersion which wouldn't do much for anybody if it didn't, however, come through with an easy, an uninsistent (as it hopes) but functioning net of detail. Detail such as, in this poem, the "kids" with their "stipendium-years in Paris," a pattern which is a familiar one in Stockholm, as it is in other Scandinavian towns; the "bigtime tennis in Båstad," a noticeable July event in those parts; Strandvägen, the indeed-elegant street with its facades and its mostly white sailboats and yachts, all of them pointed towards the summer islands—these and more.

That's part of it, of what I think makes the poem work. The other part is what I started with up at the top of the page: the felt presence of time. This gets to wherever it gets through its details, but now it's the detailed admissions of memory, literature's primal hoard, having to do, here, with its own (as it surely knows it must be, or it's done for) cache of images, viz., roads-not-brought-into-headlights, milky-skinned redheads and glimpses on escalators, also unobserved seasons and "necessary" but unspoken sentences, all from the same shared-by-billions instinct but each appearance of it, here, as it intends, signalling in its newness, towards lost time.

What you say about the "detailed admissions of memory" is interesting. How does that follow through in a poem like "Photograph in a Stockholm Newspaper for March 13, 1910"?

Good question, and one which brings home to me that it's a good thing I didn't claim that every one of my poems had any obvious relationship at all to memory—only the unavoidable, off-stage, unconfessed relationship that memory has to everything we do. (A few years ago, my son met, for a few minutes in Saigon, an elderly guy whose usual address was the same small town in Western Ontario where a great-uncle of that son had spent his life; learning my son's surname, this man told him that he had noticed his *walk* to be identical with that of the deceased uncle. Was that just bone alignment? Or could it have been a case of much-younger son watching admired ex-athlete uncle move and building this into memory? *Vem vet*: *svensk* for "who knows")?

Back to your question's bigger point. That poem's origin was, as it says, seeing a newspaper's archival photo of a working-class, probably, family standing in a courtyard in an early 1900s moment. There's no personal memory for me in that courtyard at all; it had taken me fifty years to even arrive in the same town, half the family dead by then and the courtyard probably obliterated. What it was was a feeling I can have at any time concerning a life that apparently lived itself out modestly, unnoticeably, all its motions and words gone tracelessly, a feeling that no doubt can misjudge much and be thought to romanticize shamelessly but which just surges up in me pretty often and sometimes ends up where its subject never was and perhaps never wished to be—in print, put there as if it needed attention to be paid. Shades of Gray's plowman and Miller's salesman all in one sentence.

That feeling you describe, is it the same as the "felt presence of time" you mentioned earlier? Can you define it a bit more? Is this inspiration, if you had to give it such a name?

No, I don't think it's the same as the generic business of Time. It's an unwillingness to go along with what can, when you step back from it and take a hard, fresh look at it, be seen as a brutal primeval agreement (what sort of halfway-sensitive creature could have put, on behalf of all of us, his or her signature to *this*?) that *this* is the rhythm the world is going to move to: things will be seen and then will be lost to sight, words will be spoken but at once succumb to silence, beings will be born and die, light will grow and then fade, all these will go, they're already gone, just now they were here but no more. *Why should this be?* Listing all these and trying not to flop into bathos, trying to keep a little freshness at the list's edges, what's in play here includes, well, *everything*: for example, a sentence that some cared-about person spoke years ago that one should have paused longer at, one was just realizing the need for this when, look, it's only just now that it was being said but nothing's being done about it, and now, don't even look, it's gone *forever*. Or it could be something visual, a scene glimpsed in its waiting stillness, how perfect, how long had it been waiting, you'd had no preparation for this, and when you went back, it was not the same. Or it's a turn of a head, a glance that was offered and may have been huge with unrecoverable portent. Who can bear this? Everyone. *Verweile doch, Du bist so schön.* We cope with this as best we can. Cope via diaries and scrapbooks and toys in the attic. Making art.

In your poems, in a way that's related to what you've just said, it occurs to me that it's the work of art—material culture and the object in itself—that is central. This brings to mind *The Prinzhorn Collection*—a collection not easily canonized—or even *My Death as the Wren Library.*

I think it's an interesting matter to raise. I also think it's being much done these days—this insertion into a poem or into any other art piece of substantial material from elsewhere, sometimes well managed, often not. I think *Prinzhorn* is a fringe member of this sort of assembly. There's a lot of lines directly presented—in that poem, in their original German, in the written words of the man locked into that asylum for all those years—and it's important that these words are there, that they're in the poem in their unchanged form, just as he wrote them in those letters which his keepers never mailed, which his family never saw. It was important to me, to have them among the words I was adding to them, that I was locating them among. Making it at least possible that now, finally, a few people would read them. They had led me to my poem, and they resonate, I believe, inside the poem; they convince me the poem can dare to matter.

Wren relates rather less to this, I'd think. That poem came directly, some of it came word for word, from a dream, during a sabbatical year in Cambridge, where I was writing every weekday from 9 a.m. (after I'd walked my small son to school) to about 3 in the afternoon, six hours a day unlunched. I'm convinced that it was this near-total immersion in poem writing that permitted, facilitated, this dream, where I dreamed in near-stanza form and woke one morning at 3 or 4 o'clock and had the good sense to write the dreamed images down and even to be given, by my dream, the *lineation* for some of those words. So there's a borrowing and a putting-to-use not unrelated to your thought of the "solid work of art": in this case, I'm not borrowing from another person's work of art; I'm borrowing from a source which I never did attribute to my own skill or hard work but simply to this gift from a dream (I could never—never—have come up with the thought of my "death" turning "me" into "the Wren library in Trinity's Neville's court," let alone my dream-friend's immortal (to me) line "oh my little bicycle," which more than one correspondent has told me is a line she (two women, in fact) loves above all. I like it too, but I have only a tangential right to it.

Any thoughts as to why so many of your poems take up from others' work? Can we call this inspiration? Ekphrasis?

When I run over a number of such poems or poem moments (I haven't thought how many there might be), I decide that it has very often happened (and often happened with no poem follow-up, no traceable echo) that a writer I'm reading (or often, though less so than in that first case, a piece of visual art, and even more rarely—though now and then—a piece of music, à la Proust's petit phrase) touches me in a way that takes me deeper into myself than anything in the most recent weeks of my everyday life has taken me. And may then lead to a poem of my own. The most recent event along this line (though it hasn't led anywhere in my own writing and may never) was re-reading a passage in W.G. Sebald's *The Rings of Saturn*, which I'd read years ago and liked, but initially liked less than his *The Emigrants* (I was sent back to *The Rings* by James Wood's Sebald essay), and finding a passage of such beauty (it felt unrivalled by anything I'd read or written for years—maybe this was an overreaction, maybe it will find a more sober place in a while, though maybe not). This kind of thing doesn't invite emulation in any content sense, but it does starkly remind one of a level of aim, of ambition, that one should remember and demand of oneself—whether one ever gets there or not isn't the point, but the knowledge that it exists, that it has been humanly achieved, and not too long ago either, not merely in ancient tyme in an Urn Burial or a seldom-thought-on Shakespeare history play.

This sort of thing has led to a Beckett-related poem which you'll know of; and there's Keats, and I'm not sure how many more.

The influences and interests you describe in *A Dropped Glove in Regent Street* are mostly European (Borges perhaps being the great exception). At one point, you write that "a great many writers from this country [Canada] or the one to the south of us, spend half of every year in

Europe." Can you say a bit more about your connection to Europe?

My sense of a close relationship to Europe is a secure one, and I don't find this (apart from those odd hours which contain an unscheduled stab of longing for, say, Covent Garden and the usually empty Inigo Jones's church so close by, or, in Cambridge, the path beside a very small stream running alongside Trinity's tennis courts, or a high-up flat over the Malar sea in Stockholm or... like that) anything other than a plus in my life. Two excuses for this, one of which I've just indicated: I spent my twenties and half of my thirties in one or other European cities, and these are years when, if the world is ever going to open its arms to you, these will be the right ones, and for me it did, and they were. Nothing new about that, although stuff lingers.

And then there's art, both visual and literary. The former category points, for me, at Edvard Munch in Norway and Masaccio's *Expulsion from the Garden* in Florence and the endless high-ceilinged walkway of the Kunsthistorisches Museum in Vienna—and points also at the twenty or thirty mornings I spent, miraculously and with minimal talent, at the St. Martin's School of Art on Charing Cross Road in a life-drawing class of a dozen girls or women and three boys or men, seven of whom, this is the mentioned miracle, almost at once entered one another's lives with a vitality and a kind of serious promise which I, so time-confused now when I recall them in their abiding youth that I really shouldn't be permitted to remember them at all, nevertheless remember and, it seems, love. Love more awarely than I did way back then.

And yes, books. "I think that Heaven," Virginia Woolf wrote in her diary, "will be composed of endless and untiring reading," and although I once found her "untiring" incomprehensible (who needed heavenly help to read tirelessly?), that was when I could read all day and half the night, happy with what I was up to and, I suppose, content to know that the rest of the world was falling into what another great writer, Nabokov, called "the moronic fraternity of sleep." That was then and this is now, but reading remains my sine qua non: every bit as good and far more reliable than even a decent-level two-out-of-three sets of tennis doubles (much as I have cared for those several thousand sets). And this has just about always meant, for me, the reading of *European* writers, with regard to whom I take the author of *Hamlet* as nonpareil and then recommence our conversation with Tolstoy, who has very recently survived, no problem, my sixth immersion in the two masterpieces, and who, for me, obliterates every other fiction writer to a degree that I wish he would not (though there've been dozens of others of great worth, some of them predictable (George Eliot, Samuel Beckett, Chekhov, Turgenev, Thomas Mann) and others perhaps less obvious (Heinrich Böll, all of his touching and simple novels read in German, and individual wonderfulnesses such as Constant's *Adolphe* and Flaubert's *Un Coeur Simple* and sideshelves of shaky but fondly-browsed-in add-ons like Cyril Connolly's *The Unquiet Grave*. And the poetry of Rilke and Keats and Housman and Milton and Edward Thomas and Larkin. And about forty volumes of literary biography by people like Tomalin and Holmes and Maddox and MacCarthy).

Gertrude Stein writes in a journal that "America will be a good place for writers sometime, but not yet," and I'm not in the mood to amplify or justify this but will only nod my sixty-years-later head in agreement.

OK, I'll add just this much. Having a thousand and more years of invoked memory available to you on a walk through any familiar wood, or down (not all, admittedly, but many) centuries-trodden streets, gazing across battle-historied fields or waters or the silhouette of a medieval town, turning pages in a book which has endured the touch of Gibbon or Goethe—matters. It can deepen a day's thoughts.

Following up on all the talk about your connection to Europe: How do you see your interests and influences fitting into Canadian poetry? Are you a Europhile Canadian?

"Europhile" sounds a bit tidy, though there's no question I read more European writers than Canadian, ratio a lot to one. I'm pretty sure many Canadian writers do the same. I read the *Guardian* every Saturday and have more pleasure and lasting worth from one of those than from a month of anything close to home. I've never travelled to or in any continent other than Europe, which I'm sure is my loss but I can live with it. On the slightly other hand, I've never wished to have been born anywhere but Woodstock, Ontario, to have had parents other than the two remarkable ones I had, or to have had teachers, at the college level, other than Northrop Frye and Marshall McLuhan in Toronto, both of whom I had lots of hours with and never found their equal in, say, Cambridge. Nobody even close.

With regard to your first question up there, one kind of answer might be that

I've directed many, many creative-writing groups at York University and in assorted other places and colleges and high schools, and given readings in almost every province of my country; and I did those six-week sessions at Banff for those ten years, meeting many youngish Canadian writers and working with them on their poetry and once in a while on their prose, and enjoying almost every minute of all of those times. And I suppose "interests and influences" might be involved here. This may not be a subtle response; on the other hand, perhaps it at least shows a degree of modesty, and about time too.

Throughout *A Dropped Glove…*, you also write of likeable, honourable men: Orwell, Chekhov, Kafka, your father. Why is this so important?

I don't know that I have much more to say about this except that among the writers you list, all are exceptional in their art or sullen craft as well as likeable and honourable men. I'd put Samuel Beckett at or near the top of any such group, by the way—never mind *Godot*, if you read his letters, written in his twenties when he is for the first time travelling about the continent (of Europe!) and is commenting on the paintings, the galleries he's been visiting, you're bound to be moved by this very young man's sophisticated judgments, the unselfconscious daring of these, and "likeable" and "honourable," both those, suggest themselves to me all the way through. There are also, or there were, as of course you know, gifted writers of another persuasion, writers who exploited or betrayed anyone who strayed near them: Canetti for one, and there are more but *passons*; and then there are people like Proust and Rilke, who were, both of them, as close to genius as any except the above-hymned Tolstoy and Shakespeare, but neither of whom I'd much want to buddy up with. Otherwise, and in general, my reasons for caring about "honourable" men are without originality: one learns, I think, to care more about a word like this as one lives longer and learns how rarely it's justified. Maybe I'm simply admiring my betters in both their art and their lives.

And your father?

Fitting my father into a paragraph centring on honour, on what is honourable, is in some ways no problem. Thirty years after his death, he is, for me and for starters, easy to be unambivalently fond of. He was, I think, not a complex man: he was sixteen years old in a small town in Ontario when World War I began, and he was in the trenches near Arras when it ended, and although he marched through those small-town streets with the other vets on the anniversaries of Armistice Day when I was too young to know what was up, he never, even much later, had a lot to say about all that. Not about that and not about, I quite often felt, much else either. Words weren't his thing. When both my brother and I became published academics, he knew how many books there were, but other than that, not much; and he didn't really want to be told. You didn't talk about what you'd accomplished; that was bad form. It was a code. Sometimes this felt OK, it was so *not* the continual palaver, on the page or aloud, that you and your likes kept on with. Other times, it felt boring. Basically, it's that last that oppressed me, but here's another story, a tennis story which my dad, a gifted athlete, naturally wouldn't approve of me telling, a story which links him with, scary partnership, the great Orientalist Edward Said. Said had a letter in the *LRB* years ago in which he pointed out that tennis nowadays was remote from what it had been in his own warmly remembered tennis-playing years; the millions of available dollars and the year-round cashing in on those millions had moved it far from the real world; there was no longer the remotest connection between the game the Samprases were playing and the game old guys like my contemporary Edward Said had played and this was a loss. I wrote to agree with him and told the story, which *LRB* readers also got to read, of the English Davis Cup team barnstorming in Ontario in the 1920s and, when they reached Jack Coles's hometown, needing a replacement for one of their two singles contests. Jack Coles was the local number one, knew he would be outgunned, decided therefore to go for every line and hit every ball as hard as he could, got lucky and … won the match. There was no way, my letter concluded, that this could happen nowadays. This may strike you as having little to do with honour, but it's part of my picture of this man, that he could do this Homeric, high-noon thing and tell the story only (at least in my hearing) once, a story

I'd have amplified and told dozens of times if I'd had such news ready to go. Large-scale verb though it may be that's coming next here, I honour him for the difference.

Oh, one more thing that he did. He admired my mother all the days of their life together. She deserved every day of it, which doesn't make his awareness of it any less worth honouring.

You also quote Cyril Connolly: "For me to love the poem is to love the poet who wrote it and become his man."

Whether it's a poet or some other kind of writer, it's not a line I would sign my name to. It evokes, for me, a query I once put to myself in an idle moment—I asked myself how much it mattered to me that I had never met Albert Camus, never heard him read, never had the chance to tell him how, on my first reading of a remembered page of the first of his books (*L'Etranger*, a thin book which, for its clarity and its swiftness and also for its thinness, was carried about in my back pocket for most of a Paris summer long ago, the first summer of the book's life and the twentieth of mine), two sentences moved out of their paragraph and gave me a minute or so's feeling of something I had no experience of and no definition for but knew was special, knew that the two sentences had halted the usual haphazard running of the film of my life and were now letting me know, or guess, or half-understand, with a sort of, possibly (the word I'm choosing to use next here could ruin all this, I know, but try not to let it do that), *wonder*, that two average-length sentences could do this, that I was now in an unusual mind-state which these sentences had, without a syllable of warning, effected, achieved, for me. I was, I think, startled that this was a thing you could do, that the little echoes that these words were mutually and perfectly offering and receiving inside their lines could do this. But that's *all* it was. It was the words, the lines, the little thin book. It wasn't the man; it was what he had in a special hour, or in twenty tries over two weeks, made.

In light of the admission in this conversation that among my favourite readings are literary biographies, the above paragraph might seem a non sequitur. But I don't think it is. Learning, and wanting to learn, details of the life and work habits of the author of a book or books which one likes very much does not mean one is en route to liking or (tired-of-life word) loving that author. It doesn't mean one is willing to "become his man." There's a plethora of reasons why this is so, it seems to me. Some other day.

Your most recent collection, *Where We Might Have Been*, is linked, through many of the poems, to *A Dropped Glove in Regent Street*. Some of your recollections in the latter become poems in the former. Do many of your poems develop this way, from prose?

I'm sure I've done this a few times, don't know how often. I'm not anxious to overdo the tactic; it can, I think, limit the freedom of movement of the coming poem, predetermine or inhibit its form, narrow or shape it in ways which the poem won't benefit from. And I'm not just talking about format here but about the effect of an existing piece of writing, to which one is returning for, one hopes, a good reason (for example, because one feels that that prose piece's theme or central image hasn't been exploited as it ought, the investigation has halted before it should have done), on the writer's imagination. It's as if, in using that prose source, you don't have the totally unblemished white page in front of you; the page bears traces or stains of an origin or map which is other than your best-case uncharted movement into a poem. But I'm straying from your question: the shortest and bluntest answer to "Do many of your poems develop this way, from prose?" would be "Not many, and I think I've never deliberately headed back towards my own published prose on a generalized hunt for a poem; when it's happened, it's emerged out of an unpremeditated browse." It's clear that the prose most likely to play this sort of role, that is, prose that can seem profligate in this regard, littered with unwritten poems, will of course vary with whoever's reading it. To mention one such writer, one who has mattered in this regard to me and also, a sure bet, to hundreds of others, poets and more, there's the collected correspondence of Rainer Maria Rilke, one of the twentieth century's finest poets but a man who also wrote thousands of letters, hundreds of which have been published in countless translations; and these are letters wherein you can not only find the stirrings of what would later become poems of Rilke's own but other stirrings too, incipient thoughts which he lost interest in or simply failed to return to and here they now are, signalling to you of what's kept so still so long.

Writers who can function in this way for you or for me are unlikely to be of the same name for both of us, but with luck and the requisite thousands of hours of reading, there are trouvailles of this nature for us all.

Can I ask about your process with a poem? You are known for reworking published poems. How do you see a poem after publication?

I think there's not a single poem of mine which, if its publisher advised me that they wanted a re-issue and offered me a chance to edit it, would 'scape whipping. Even if it were only a line ending or the replacing of a comma with a semicolon, let alone the more inviting chance to go for one line in place of a stanza, or the even happier prospect of entirely omitting one or more poems from the collection … done deal. I know that not everyone thinks this a good or even a tolerable way to behave: reviewers have now and then regretted that *Ur*-versions of poems of mine didn't really exist; Christopher Levenson, for instance, in a generally friendly review, contrasted a newly arrived version of a poem with an earlier one he'd liked better. But I tend to have one copy of each of my books which has got pencilled improvements on every third or so page, and these altered versions maintain their position over the years. These pages of mine become even more cluttered as time passes, but I think they never return to that first version. So, I'm not sentimental here, I don't "see a poem after publication" as having achieved any status that puts it out of reach of whatever growth or change I may have undergone.

Before we end, what are your impressions of Tomas Tranströmer winning the Nobel Prize?

Part of the problem (I've been reading more negative comments on his Nobel than the other sort, mostly about aged Swedish jurors and how the reporter had never heard of TT and seemed pleased to say so) is that TT doesn't translate easily. His use of Swedish is exceptionally calm and understated and, in this quiet which is its own creation, immensely persuasive. I have—as you know but the critics I've read do not—published a book of my translations of a very late collection called *For the Living and the Dead*, a bilingual edition published by Buschekbooks in Ottawa (it won a prize for the best translation of its year in Canada, the first time that a non-French/English book had won), and I did this translation because I had been singularly moved by Tomas's poems for decades. I don't think there's been a worthier Nobelist for a long while.

Let Me Be a Waterfall

ELISE PARTRIDGE

Elise Partridge was born in 1958 and raised near Phila-
delphia. A dual citizen of Canada and the United States,
she lived in Vancouver from 1992. She studied at Harvard
University, Cambridge University (where she was a Mar-
shall Scholar), Boston University, and the University of Brit-
ish Columbia. Her first collection, *Fielder's Choice* (2002),
was a finalist for the Lampert Award for the best first book
of poems in Canada; her second, *Chameleon Hours* (2008),
was a finalist for the British Columbia Book Prize and
won the Canadian Authors Association Poetry Prize. She
taught literature and writing at a number of universities,
including Boston, Brandeis, and the University of British
Columbia, and to immigrants in Vancouver. She died in
February 2015. *The If Borderlands: Collected Poems* was
published posthumously in 2017. This interview was begun
on October 13, 2012, and was conducted when Partridge
was living, by turns, in Vancouver and New York City.

I want to begin by asking about illness and writing—and more generally about illness and literature. I'm thinking specifically about the poems in section two in *Chameleon Hours*, the prognosis, the surgery, the side effects, the questions that you raise and never answer in your own poems about these things.

The fiction writer Peter Taylor, among others, said writing is a way of making sense of the world, and it can certainly be a way of making sense of what's happening to you if you're undergoing something especially bewildering or overwhelming—a sudden diagnosis with an uncertain prognosis, for example. If you wonder how much time you have left, or you can be sure you don't have much time, that might also spur you to write. Walter Jackson Bate has made an eloquent case for Keats's development having been hastened by his tuberculosis.

I'm not comparing myself to Keats by any means, or Taylor, but the initial drafts of the poems you ask about in *Chameleon Hours* came rushing out in the first few months after my treatment for cancer. (I wasn't able to write during treatment because the chemo affected my brain and made me anemic, so I was often foggy and fatigued.) The poems in my first book, *Fielder's Choice*, had developed very slowly, over about a decade.

I did revise the "cancer" poems many times before they eventually appeared in *Chameleon Hours*. Many of them were, I saw in retrospect, a way of trying to make sense of what had been happening to me. The situation did raise a lot of questions which were unanswerable—the inevitable

"Why did this happen?", "How long might I survive?", "What will life be like now?" Since my prognosis was uncertain, it made me think about death, of course, and whether or not there was an afterlife. Whitman says in "Goodbye, My Fancy," a valedictory poem he wrote when he was older, "Strong is thy hold O mortal flesh / Strong is thy hold, O love." I think the idea of life being cut short was so painful that that coloured some of what I said in the poems. When I re-read these recently, I realized my pictures of an afterlife with my husband, for example, came out of what felt like an almost unbearable grief about and fear of being separated from him through death.

A potentially fatal illness can make you want to use your time more wisely in general, and to keep changing and developing, which gave rise to the title poem in the collection. It's dedicated to one of my brothers who is extraordinarily energetic and curious about everything. A shift in priorities after cancer is quite common too. That's behind the poem "Farewell Desires." I finally understood more about the freedom and lightness that comes from not clinging to things or feelings or states of mind.

The illness made me very grateful for the many friends and family members who had tried in various ways to help, which is what "Granted a Stay" is partly about. And finally, within a year, I saw young women I had met through a group at the BC Cancer Agency, where I was treated, some of whom had better prognoses than I did, suffer recurrences or die of their cancer. It was very difficult. I wrote elegies for my friends.

As I mentioned, the poems rushed out, and I hesitated about publishing the ones that were about me. Isaac

Bashevis Singer said that anyone who talks about himself too much is a nudnik. I asked family, friends, mentors, and editors whether the poems seemed too merely personal. My eventual hope was that some of them could even be useful to someone in a similar situation: for example, my poems about chemotherapy side effects. I'm not sorry I had the chemotherapy, as it was suggested it would help save my life, and it's not a happy situation for any cancer patient to dread the side effects, but I also found that it helped me to learn more about them from someone who'd experienced them. That provided one possible justification for publishing poems like these.

What you say about the "rushing out" of poems and about "Farewell Desires" brings me to a line from that poem: "let me be a waterfall / pouring a heedless mile." Yet, as a writer, you are anything but heedless, your published poems nothing like an outpouring. Can you say something about this?

The wish I mentioned here was about trying to be authentic, unencumbered, and generous—to live headlong without clinging to things I might sometimes think I wanted, much less to the trivial; about life being constantly unpredictable, and wanting to live with as much spontaneity and vitality as possible. The poem did grow out of the illness, though the wish had been there before; I think perhaps the illness made it stronger. After wondering whether or not my life was going to end much earlier than it might have otherwise, naturally I had to think about how I wanted to live from then on. Things I had wanted to happen were not going to happen, because of the cancer, and this at first seemed catastrophic; and yet other things that turned out to be important did happen because of the cancer. This put paid to the idea that one can always trust what one wishes for. Nobody would wish to have cancer, yet it undeniably brought things to my life that were, to my great surprise, valuable. Also, after having been so ill, I found I wanted to be bolder about many experiences. Fearing one might be deprived of chances can of course motivate one to take more chances. The heedlessness was about being freer—not constraining oneself in any defeating way—and simultaneously about being "freer" in the medieval sense of the word: open-handed, generous.

As for not being heedless in terms of writing poetry, I sometimes wish I could work faster, but most of the poems I eventually publish take me a long time to finish. There are a couple of remarks I keep in mind about being heedful. Szymborska was once asked why she hadn't published more. She replied, "I have a trashcan in my house." And then there's Théophile Gautier: "Anything which is not well made doesn't exist."

At the end of "For a Father," the children or perhaps the family itself are "straggling behind, shouting, *Wait*—." In "The Runt Lily," the speaker is, among other things, waiting for a flower to bloom. And in "Since I Last Saw You," "The crane was waiting in the marsh… / …carried you away." Can you say a bit about waiting in these poems?

"For a Father," in the first two stanzas, is about children trying to keep up with a youthful and energetic father, asking him to wait as he dashes from one thing to the next. In the third stanza, the father has died and the children are wishing irrationally, as children might after a death, that their father had waited before dashing off and leaving them behind, as they feel, forever.

"The Runt Lily" is partly about a friend who died much too young, of cancer. I had met her in a support group at the British Columbia Cancer Agency when we were both going through chemo. After I was first diagnosed, my brother-in-law and my husband planted some beautiful stargazer lilies in our backyard. Most of them kept blooming except for one that really seemed to be struggling. It produced a couple of buds and then was battered by a storm; eventually, it did manage one precarious flower. I didn't know, when I started the poem about this hardy lily, that it would be about Rhonda, but she quickly became the subject. It's not useful to make comparisons that are too pointed and that would strain the metaphor; my waiting for the lily to flower doesn't really correspond directly to my experience with Rhonda in the last year of her life. The similarity lay more in watching her struggle to keep thriving (she was diagnosed with an extremely aggressive cancer, and the odds were against her surviving from the start) and in being inspired by how stubbornly she kept her strength until the end. Those last months were of course agonizing for her, especially because she had young children. The last year of her life was like a vigil for many of us who knew her, and yet she kept going with remarkable energy, courage, and humour. The vibrancy of this afflicted flower must have reminded me of her.

"Since I Last Saw You" is about another friend I met through that cancer support group, Gabi Helms, and for whom there was also a kind of vigil at the end. She originally seemed to have good chances for survival. But her cancer returned a few years after she'd finished her treatment, when she was several months pregnant with her first child. The doctors knew the minute they found the metastases that, barring a miracle, she could die anytime. She desperately wanted to stay alive at least long enough so the child could be born. She suffered horribly for weeks in the hospital as she tried to hang on, through an arduous chemo regimen, till the child came closer to term. The child survived, but Gabi never regained consciousness after her daughter was born. In many Asian works of literature, the crane is a symbol of longevity, and there's a legend for example about a crane taking a Taoist immortal to the afterlife. I admired Gabi; she'd led the organization of the first conference in Canada for young women with breast cancer, and I saw her as a kind of immortal.

All of what you've described in those poems connects the notion of waiting to sickness and death. But illness, you've said earlier, makes you want to use your time more wisely.

The waiting in "The Runt Lily" is more an anxiety and eagerness to see the life flourish against odds. The crane's waiting in the marsh in "Since I Last Saw You" is, I suppose, an emblem for how difficult it can be to accept a loss; the idea that the crane is on a kind of death watch, but so the dying person can be taken to an afterlife, is perhaps one way I was trying to comfort myself about Gabi's death. I wouldn't write a similar poem now, as I've come to reject the idea of an actual afterlife, though I feel people's lives continue to some degree through friends and family and through their work. The urging the father in the poem to "wait" is an urging not to be left behind in all kinds of ways, a plea for companionship.

To take this a bit further, having read your commentary on those three poems, it seems to me what all three have at their centre is compassion—and part of that is waiting and patience. Can you say something about this compassion?

Funny you should say that, as patience in everyday life has never been one of my virtues. I hate waiting in lines, for example, and always have something to read in case I'm trapped in one. I instinctively associate waiting with passivity and helplessness, not with stoicism, for example, though of course I recognize that many forms of waiting do involve fortitude. But when it comes to waiting in general, I prefer motion, action, progress whenever possible.

These poems are simply about people I knew. To see the tragedy that befell Rhonda and Gabi was searing for everyone around them. Watching how people reacted actually taught me a lot about compassion and love. Homo homini lupus, yes, but after seeing what I saw, I don't think it's sentimental to say that humans are also very strongly bound to each other through love and tenderness.

The father in the poem you mention was a person whose sense of fun was contagious and who also died relatively young, though in very different circumstances. I suppose the emotion in that poem is related to how much joy he had taken in life at times and to the plea not to depart from the children who wanted to go on participating in that joy with him.

In your "Sisyphus: The Sequel," the existential struggle comes to an end with the rock stopped at the top of the hill and the mythical figure laughing, finding a new way to approach his work with a chisel. The meaninglessness and the suffering end, not because of man but because of nature. André Breton argued something similar—that it wasn't Sisyphus who was worn down by the struggle but the rock which wears over time. The notion comes up again later in *Chameleon Hours* in "Snail Halfway Across the Road," though this time the pointless struggle for safety lies "ten lifetimes ahead."

When I wrote "Sisyphus: The Sequel," I was imagining that the suffering of Sisyphus started to diminish when he accepted his burden more. In that sense, yes, he freed himself somewhat from being constantly worn down by the struggle. He wasn't so absorbed in the suffering; the experience became part of who he was.

"Snail Halfway Across the Road" centres on a battered-looking snail I watched trying to cross a road on Salt Spring

Island off British Columbia. It seemed like such a quixotic and risky thing for the snail to do, and of course it was taking a long time to accomplish. I guess that poem is about pressing forward in the face of potential or actual suffering, about how safety is always a mirage and the longing for it has to be somewhat ignored.

Your question actually helped me see how many of the poems in my first books are about suffering, explicitly or implicitly—about overcoming suffering or coping with it ("Phoenix," "Rural Route," "Farewell Desires"), about suffering in the natural world ("Caught" and "In the Barn"), or suffering brought on by social injustice ("Vuillard Interior" and "1959") or war ("Two Monuments"). Other poems are about more private suffering ("Childless," "First Death," "Chemo Side Effects: Memory").

You mentioned earlier that you've "come to reject the idea of an actual afterlife." Can you say something about your belief?

I try to address questions of belief in some of my poems, such as "One Calvinist's God," "Crux," "Gnomic Verses from the Anglo-Saxon" and "A Valediction." In "Granted a Stay," the allusions to various religious traditions refer also to the people who offered to pray for me when I was in cancer treatment. I think my childhood was somewhat unusual for where I grew up and when, in that I had a religious education—my family went to church every Sunday from the time I was very young till the time I went off to college. Our minister was an enthusiastic reader of George

Herbert, Robert Browning, and other poets who wrote about religion—I first heard Auden's name from his pulpit. In college, I took a course on the Bible and also fulfilled requirements by taking a course on church history, another on medieval Jewish and Christian thought, and so on. Finally, the biggest literary discovery I made in college was medieval literature; I loved Chaucer and Langland, and of course their work is full of references to religion. Later on, when I began a meditation practice, I started reading up on Buddhism. For many years, I really didn't know what I believed. I'm agnostic now, but I don't reject what I find wise in the Old and New Testaments and texts of other traditions.

A number of the poems in your first collection, I'm thinking especially of "Rural Route," are rural in their setting. Are you a farm girl?

No, I grew up in a leafy suburb. I was lucky to have a friend who grew up further out in the countryside, and at one point, I had family living near a regional park where I saw some of the other things I wrote about in that book. "Rural Route" was about the family of a friend who had grown up quite far out in the country. After I moved to British Columbia, I wanted to learn more about its flora, fauna, and ecology; I also regularly looked after a farmhouse for a friend on Salt Spring Island, and some of what I read, heard, and saw there found its way into poems.

When and where did you study with Lowell?

In the spring of 1977, I took two courses with Robert Lowell at Harvard, when I was a freshman there. One was a seminar on nineteenth-century English and American poets, the other a writing workshop that also surveyed twentieth-century poets. I took voluminous notes (as was my anxious habit in all my courses). One professor I studied with later at university asked us to try a dramatic monologue; I was having trouble inventing a character and put into blank verse some of the remarks Lowell had made about various poets in those spring 1977 seminars, which the professor, to my surprise, eventually asked to publish. I hesitated about that request, because I wasn't sure how I felt about it all or how Lowell would have felt. I consulted with Robert Fitzgerald, who had also been one of my teachers and a close friend of Lowell's. He said he thought it was fine to go ahead, and I trusted his judgment. I felt grateful to all three teachers. I've also published a couple of articles on Lowell's teaching and will be working on more.

What brought you to Vancouver in 1992? What did you know about Canadian poetry when you arrived?

I came to Vancouver because my partner had been offered a job there. Before I arrived, I'd been introduced to Canadian poetry mostly through anthologies, which can be useful but which of course one has to go beyond. In the anthologies, I'd encountered Avison, Atwood, bpNichol, Birney, Klein, Layton, Ondaatje, Ormsby, Purdy, Page, Pratt, MacEwen,

Cohen, Nowlan, Waddington, and others. I'd also read some contemporary Canadian poetry via, for example, *The Fiddlehead*, a journal I've respected for a long time for its broad-minded approach.

Do you see yourself as a Canadian poet?

I'm a Canadian citizen and have now lived almost half my life in Canada. I'm grateful to Canada and admire many writers here; both its general and literary culture have influenced me a good deal. The question of a national identity isn't at the forefront necessarily when I'm sitting at my desk, something I realized when this issue came up with a friend. Recently, I'd asked four Canadian poets if they'd be interested in participating in a panel on Canadian poetry that I wanted to organize for a conference in the States. As we were discussing what title to give the panel, one of the poets—someone who's lived in Canada all her life and written eloquently about Canadian landscapes and art—said, "When I write, I don't think of myself as a Canadian poet." Although, having lived in three different cultures, I'm very aware of how societies shape their inhabitants, when I'm actually writing, I'm also not considering this particular question. I wonder as well if there would be presumption involved in my calling myself a Canadian poet when I grew up elsewhere. I would say that the categorizations, if they're an issue, have to be made by others. I'm reminded of a jazz band called the Either/Orchestra and of the suggestive possibilities for me in that name and in what they do (that is, drawing on various influences in the music they play

and the approach they take). Does one have to be either/
or in terms of a national identity—or can one be a hybrid
making some kind of orchestral noise out of one's mingled
heritages and experiences? Why not?

So Foreign Here

STEVEN HEIGHTON

Steven Heighton was born in 1961 in Toronto and grew up there and in the small town of Red Lake in Northern Ontario. From 1988 to 1994, he edited the influential literary magazine *Quarry*. He published seven collections—including *The Waking Comes Late* (2016), winner of the Governor General's Literary Award for Poetry, and *Selected Poems: 1983–2020* (2021)—and four novels—*The Shadow Boxer* (2000); *Afterlands* (2005), a *New York Times Book Review* Editors' Choice; *Every Lost Country* (2010); and *The Nightingale Won't Let You Sleep* (2017). In 2011, he published *Workbook: Memos and Dispatches on Writing*. A book of short stories, *Instructions for the Drowning*, appeared posthumously in 2023. He died in April 2022. This interview was begun in August 2013. Heighton lived in Kingston, Ontario.

I'd like to start by asking about history—an important feature of your poems. How do you prepare/research for a poem like "The Machine Gunner"? Or "Selected Monsters"?

For the most part, I don't. I'm not being glib or coy about this. The truth is, much as I respect scholarship, I'm lazy and impatient when it comes to research.

I realize that many writers love to do background research and some even prefer it to the creative work that follows. For me, the labour of poring over sources and taking down and organizing careful notes is too much like being back in school and completing an assignment. Still, I value accuracy, especially at the level of concrete detail, so I do research my work when I have to, but usually not till after I've written several drafts. I call it retro-research.

Of course, a writer has to set out with *some* knowledge of a subject, as I did with the historical anecdote at the heart of "Selected Monsters" (in 1460, Cosimo de' Medici arranged for various animals, including a giraffe, of all things, to be brought into an arena to fight each other, to determine which was the most ferocious). But I happen to think that a bare modicum of knowledge is enough, maybe even ideal. Run with what you know and imagine the rest. Don't let pre-researched facts throttle your options. Novelists and poets need not be compliant clerks to reality. (Disclaimer: this attitude might be nothing but a rationalization of laziness.)

As for the "retro-research": when the exhilarating first-draft rush is over, and while embarked on the slower, more onerous process of later-draft revision, I do research as necessary, to see where I got it wrong, and then I correct accordingly— so long as the "correction" doesn't violate the spirit of what evolved during the first draft. (I find that if I've managed to write my way into that zone where the work seems to author itself—a state of absorption, of self-forgetting engagement—my imagination will have gotten it right most of the time. If I haven't managed to enter that zone, later factual corrections are beside the point, since the work will be dead on the page.)

A concrete example. In the bullring, presided over by de Medici and the pope, were a lion, a bull, a bloodhound, a gorilla, and a giraffe. (To the crowd's disappointment, the baffled contestants declined to fight.) If while working on the poem I'd decided that instead of a bloodhound I needed a more totemic beast, like a wolf—whether for symbolic reasons or because the word "wolf" better fit my prosody (the poem is consonantally end-rhymed, and "wolf" might have paired with life/half/gulf/self, etc.)—I would have shape-shifted the dog to suit my purposes with no scruple.

It seems to me that there is no distinct place for your history—there are poems set during the wars, during the Renaissance, in early twentieth-century America, in Japan, or ancient Greece. What attracts you to different historical settings?

Two main things. First, I'm drawn by narratives of injustice, as in the anecdote above (the issue in that case being our habit of inflicting atrocities on the natural world). Second, especially in my fiction, I seem to be engrossed by stories in which a small, diverse group of people are isolated and forced together into a struggling microcosm. I see my last three novels—including the one I'm now working on—as a sort of trilogy of such narratives. The new book is wholly imagined, but the first two, *Afterlands* and *Every Lost Country*, are loosely based on real events, the first of which happened in the Arctic in the 1870s and the second in the Himalayas in 2006.

In your *Workbook*, you define a writer as "someone trying to extend childhood—its exuberant creativity, its capacity for timeless absorption—all the way to death, thus bypassing adulthood altogether." Yet you also note that "intense creativity" is a joy because it "integrates an adult's productive powers with the playful oblivion of a child." Can you say a bit more about the connection between the childhood imagination, the extending of it through adulthood?

I'm obsessed with these issues, as the partial contradiction between those two memos suggests. (Contradictory convictions, if they're not just a symptom of shaggy thinking, usually flag a node of obsession in the mind.) I just re-watched Guillermo del Toro's masterpiece *Pan's Labyrinth*, and it struck me that one of the film's conceptual oppositions involves historical time—the unhappy realm that adults inhabit, at least while they're not asleep—and sacramental time, eternity, the realm of nature, early childhood and the dreaming mind. I've heard it said that we're all geniuses while dreaming. I would add this corollary: given that small children spend much of their waking time (or used to) in a state close to dreaming—the same state that artists need to tap into while working—the child shares the genius of the dreamer. Anyway, if as an artist you've managed to remain childlike, that turnstile to eternity is easier to access and pass through.

I'm a man who wants to live as a child—a bit like my Greek mother—but who was also raised, by an old-school ex–naval officer father, to be stoically, responsibly, chrono-centrically "adult." I've come to value both modes, but I think I would have been content to remain a selfishly creative child if it weren't for becoming a parent myself. As a parent, you do have to grow up—or at least moonlight as an adult. It's a truth that terrified me at first. I figured that "parent-mind"—preoccupied with schedules, routines, logistics, crossing chores off lists, and caring for others—would be bad for the work, and in some ways, of course it is, because it devours so much time and keeps hauling you out of the sacramental mode and back into the logistical/secretarial.

But on the whole, I was wrong. As with any parent who doesn't hate the job, my vision of life and, hence, my imaginative scope have widened hugely with fatherhood. Being a parent, and thus an adult, alters your vision of time and mortality. You can't help starting to see yourself as part of a vast and communal enterprise, instead of a discrete, isolate being—an eternal child enwombed at the navel of the cosmos. Eternal children can write nothing but lyric poems until their lyric source is depleted; or else they write self-focused, first-person Bildungsromans, one or two at the most, till that source too dries up. A child who becomes an adult—even if an incomplete, part-time, sometimes grudging one—is inducted into the world's larger life and can never run out of material.

The biographical elements you mention about your parents bring me nicely to notions of mother tongue and to your interests in translation. In "Portrait of a Mother," you write: "so foreign here, you were, your bones / not marrowed with frost." A connection and disconnection.

I should clarify that while my mother was Greek, Greek was not my mother tongue. Greek was all around me when I was a child, but so was English, and English predominated. But it gets more complicated, because I was immersed early in several unusual kinds of English: the Anglo-Saxon and Middle English that my father, a high school and uni-versity literature teacher, often recited in lieu of lullabies or bedtime stories. And after quoting, say, certain lines in Anglo-Saxon from *Beowulf*, he would translate into modern English: "Bid men of battle / build me a barrow / High above Hronesness…" Or he would ham up the opening of Chaucer's Prologue to *The Canterbury Tales* and then gloss the full sense and footnote the many words I didn't know. Then there was his theatrically burred cover of "The Ballad of Sir Patrick Spens." I soon got a sense of the English language not as a stable, finished, neatly bordered entity but a sprawling, living, mutating thing … a many-mouthed monster.

Come to think of it, during the Greek Orthodox masses I attended as a child, I came to realize the same thing about Greek, because my mother, albeit fluent in modern Demotiki, couldn't understand or explain to me some of the liturgical Greek the priest would intone. Nor could she read newspapers in Greece in the late '60s, when we visited, because the fascist regime of the colonels was forcing all newspapers to publish in the artificial Katharevousa (roughly, "cleansed Greek"). Languages, clearly, were polyvalent and labyrinthine, not unified and monolithic.

I wonder now if in some ways that perception was daunting to me as a child. I wonder if one of the reasons I became obsessed with translation, both as metaphor and as actual practice, is that it seemed a way to impose order on chaos, that churning crucible of tongues and dialects? Of course, that's just retro-speculation. What I can tell you for sure is that translation is now a staple part of my writing process—a way to keep schooling myself in the craft, keep apprenticing myself to great poets. Spend a few months reading, re-reading, translating, and tinkering with a great poem in French or Latin and you've pushed yourself through a master class with whatever poet you choose, alive or a hundred generations dead. I love the challenge of trying to smuggle meaning across frontiers of time, space, and language. To conjure the horny Catullus back to life on a page or laptop screen! Wonderful.

While at university, I spent some months happily translating passages from obscure Icelandic sagas and poems so as to satisfy the requirements of Old Norse 400, a course then offered as a token, and seemingly punitive, alternative to Critical Theory 410. So thirty years ago, you could still, just barely, avoid exposure to postmodern theory, and all my instincts told me I had to. Nowadays I have nothing against theory—it's a useful tool, or toolkit—but I think I was right to avoid it at the time. It might have made me too self-conscious about the "constructed" elements of my own persona and poetry, thus inducing a kind of paralysis through analysis at a time of life when—if you're a budding poet—it's better to work in a visceral, propulsive, and unreflective way. Plenty of time for self-reflective cogitation later, when you're older and the pondering comes naturally. Ecstasy first, skepticism later; eventually, with luck, you find the balance.

You often wear masks in your poems: Borges, Catullus, Sahtouris, soldiers, Renaissance noblemen, murderers. All these different masks add up, suggest a lineage and your interests. But how different is translation from dramatic monologue?

Dramatic monologue is a sort of translation, but one involving the approximation of voice and character, as in fiction or drama, rather than approximation of form, language, and prosody.

Interesting—I think you're implying that through my choices of poems to translate I'm creating a kind of virtual monologue, an emotional autobiography told from behind a series of masks. That's a bit like the way an unfledged songbird separated from its kind will roughly reconstitute its species song by instinctively picking out the notes it needs from the songs of other species around it. (P.K. Page first used that metaphor to explain how poets develop their own voices by reading other poets and finding there the sounds and modes that their natural inclinations require. But I think the metaphor works in this sense too.)

Derek Mahon calls his translations "adaptations." Don Paterson uses the term "version," and you go for "approximations." How did you arrive at your term?

I use the term—first suggested to me by George McWhirter after he read a few of my translations—to stress that I'm staking no claim to definitiveness or authority, especially in the case of a poem from a language I can barely swear or ask directions in. In those cases, by the way, I triangulate from existing English versions, usually while consulting the original with a dictionary in hand.

There's a second reason I use the term "approximation": it functions as a loose, inclusive rubric under which I can approach translation in either a traditional "faithful" manner—trying to stay as semantically and tonally close to the original as I can—or with a more contemporary freedom and audacity.

Two of the figures in your most recent book of poems, *Patient Frame*, seem to work as opposing poles. Warrant Officer Hugh Thompson and the murderer Roy Bryant. Thompson is heroic, elegized, Bryant villainous, the subject of a dramatic monologue. "*Don't do something in hope of reward, / …it might never come*," you quote Thompson. While Bryant says, "Four thousand they paid," and gets his reward, in multiple senses. Are these two poems "rewards" in their way?

I can only hope. Because I see you're right—on one level, I was using the poems to try to confer both reward and punishment. How presumptuous—to rail against the failure of karma, to try to act as karma's deputy and step in and right two very different kinds of wrong (in Thompson's case, a heartbreaking neglect of recognition; in Bryant's case, the way he profited from his repulsive crime).

Still, if even a handful of poetry readers first heard of these men through the poems, and then looked further, my efforts weren't futile.

Let me add that if I'd been using these men as characters in a short story or a novel, I'd have complicated them morally—because I'd have had the space to complicate them. A one-page poem about someone like Thompson is simply not the right form for the task. But I wanted to commemorate the moment that he transcended his own patriotic/conservative/obedient instincts and did something remarkable. And it *was* truly remarkable— hence the hyperbole of "archangelic." I knew the word, and the tone, would bother a lot of readers and, in a way, I think that's why I did it. Pure stubbornness. A pure gamble. This is not an excuse or a justification, merely an explanation. I'm weary of irony as a default mode, and sometimes, out of pure cussedness, I push to the opposite extreme.

Then again, I'm not sure Bryant *was* morally complicated. After all, this was a man who on his deathbed was still whining that he'd only received a couple of thousand bucks for the story of his crime. No remorse. No repentance. Maybe it's a bit of a feel-good liberal myth that we're all complicated, all a mix of good and bad. It ought to be true, but maybe it isn't, not always; maybe some folks start off basically mean and just get meaner. Hence my ending to that poem, where I try to shock the liberal reader: the dying killer still rejoicing in his racist crime. By the way, the monologue came to me in a dream the night after I saw an excellent PBS documentary about the Emmett Till murder—I heard that voice speaking (no visuals) and woke up and wrote it down.

Is that something you see your poems doing (or perhaps something you'd like your poems to do): repairing past injustices?

Naturally, I would love it if my poems could perform a task that momentous. Who wouldn't? But it's a pipe dream. As I say, the best you can hope for is that you'll reach, and move, and maybe (who knows?) even change a few readers a little. Poems have done that for me.

I think back to "The Machine-Gunner" and the way in which he is both villain and hero, philosopher and soldier. Thompson and Bryant, however, are separate individuals and more clear-cut in their roles. One poem valorizes, the other condemns, where "The Machine-Gunner" doesn't pass judgment, simply observes. Can you say something about the moralistic change here? About the moral responsibility of a poet? Have your morals changed since "The Machine-Gunner"?

No. I still believe that poets and fiction writers, most of the time, should practise a sort of neutrality, simply dramatizing, or lyricizing, and leaving the ideological conclusions to readers. But sometimes these days, I choose to polemicize instead—to express a clear moral opinion in a poem—as in a recent one addressing ex-pope Benedict on the subject of clerical sex abuse and his church's cover-up. Do those poems work less well? Do they not work as poems at all? I have no idea. Only time will tell—and time, let's face it, is not likely to be kind. I mean, it seldom is to any of us, especially if we're writing "topical" poems. Well, so be it. We can only write what we feel moved and called to write. Once the work is done, we're in the poignant position of sitting alone, fingers crossed, hoping that what we had to write also happens to be what others want to read.

Finally, I want to ask about Al Purdy, about what he means to you. You write quite a bit about Purdy the man in your *Workbook*, but which poems for you are "unbeaten"?

I don't think my poetry has much in common with his on a stylistic or formal level, but I owe him a lot in terms of theme. When I first encountered his work in my early twenties, I responded strongly to poems like "Necropsy of Love," "Wilderness Gothic," and "The Country North of Belleville," poems where he was writing not just about sex and death but also about what *endures*—what transcends its historical moment. I guess I recognized those things as my own marrow-materials, and Al's success with them encouraged me to approach them in my own way. But first I had to develop a voice. Themes float in a common pool from which anyone can draw, but each voice has to be distinctive.

For me, unlike some young male poets, it wasn't hard to resist imitating Al's voice, syntax, and signature mannerisms, partly because I'd already found other acoustical models, other *musics*, that better suited my sense of rhythm and tune: poets such as Dylan Thomas, G.M. Hopkins, Sylvia Plath, W.B. Yeats, Emily Dickinson, Wilfred Owen, and P.K. Page—all in their diverse ways great acoustical technicians. Plainspokenness didn't appeal to me. It bored me. And I felt that some of my Canadian male peers, who were trying to imitate Al's *seemingly* plain voice, were really just caving in to good old North American anti-intellectualism—the fear of seeming unmanly, fussy, heady, elitist, European. I sensed something spurious in their embrace and veneration of the demotic and colloquial. I thought it a kind of inverse snobbery. When Al invented himself, he had good reason to react against the Edwardian models he'd encountered in school—and, at the same time, to find a voice that squared with his own background, class, and autodidacticism. But his middle-class, college-educated acolytes were not forging a voice under the same urgent, and solitary, pressures. They were just mimicking.

My ear longed for a richer, denser music.

In Al's best poems (*not* his best known, such as "At the Quinte Hotel," which I wish to God people would stop anthologizing and imitating, because it misrepresents his achievement), he integrated the relaxed vernacular he began developing in the 1950s with a more traditionally poetic dignity of diction and cadence. And both these qualities are assimilated into a vision and landscape that's unmistakably his own. Listen:

> Perhaps the workman's faith reaches beyond:
> touches intangibles, wrestles with Jacob,
> replacing rotten timber with pine thews,
> pounds hard in the blue cave of the sky,
> contends heroically with difficult problems of
> gravity, sky navigation and mythopoeia,
> his volunteer time and labour devoted to God,
> minus sick benefits of course on a non-union job—
>
> (from "Wilderness Gothic")

Poignancy of the Discarded

ROBYN SARAH

Robyn Sarah was born in New York City to Canadian parents and has lived most of her life in Montreal. She studied philosophy at McGill University and music at the Conservatoire du Québec, majoring in clarinet. Her poems began appearing in print in the early 1970s, and she has to date published ten collections of poetry, most recently *My Shoes Are Killing Me* (2015)—which won the Governor General's Literary Award for Poetry. She has also published a book of essays, *Little Eurekas: A Decade's Thoughts on Poetry* (2007), two collections of short stories, and a memoir, *Music, Late and Soon* (2021). In 1976, with Fred Louder, she co-founded the literary press Villeneuve Publications, publishing important early works by August Kleinzahler and A.F. Moritz, among others. She taught English at Champlain Regional College from 1975 to 1996. She has edited *The Essential George Johnston*, *The Essential Don Coles*, and *The Essential Margaret Avison* and is poetry editor for Cormorant Books. This interview was begun in May 2015.

"On Closing the Apartment of my Grandparents…" is a very intimate poem, a moment to which you invite the reader and yet it is also in its way a private moment— we learn little about the grandparents and the speaker. Intimacy and privacy at once, which shouldn't work but in your poems does. Any thoughts on this?

This is an interesting observation, and you aren't the first to make it: Margaret Avison, reviewing one of my early books, remarked that my poems "illuminate the reader's privacy without destroying the poet's." I was pleased that someone of Avison's stature had noticed and articulated so clearly what I meant to do: to allow the poem to *resonate from* my personal experience without detailing that experience too specifically, thus leaving room for a reader to hear his or her own experience in my text. I have always felt that poetry should transcend biography—that even if a poem is transparently autobiographical in origin, it should have a surface that takes it beyond the personal, a hardness as a made object, such that it ceases to be one's own and becomes everybody's: becomes public. There are many ways to do this, and I believe these constitute the art of poetry. A fellow poet, critiquing some of the new poems in *The Touchstone*, remarked in a letter to me that some readers might be disappointed at not being given "the whole story … plot, narrative, facts, emotions" behind the poems: she posited that the "expectation of gossip" is human, and legitimate in a reader of poetry. I wrote back that I distrusted the overly personal, or personally specific, in poetry, and that instead of the whole story, I thought a poem should detach itself from the biographical facts and deliver the emotional essence of the experience as a distillate—through image, sound, metaphor, and whatever formal devices best serve the purpose—evoking mood and feeling in the way that a piece of music does. This view and practice may not always be appreciated by a reading public that has extended its hunger for confessional narrative beyond prose memoir to the personal lyric. But I must write from my own sense of what a poem is.

Your comment "hardness as a made object" makes me think of a poem from your new book, *My Shoes Are Killing Me*, "Castoffs." You draw a connection here between useful and unused objects, the "intact, discarded." You clearly see a value in what others might discard. Am I safe to connect this to the value of poetry in our society? Is the birdcage without a bird like a poem without a reader?

You want to make something of that birdcage that is not what I had in mind myself, but I think it's legitimate. I gather you see the birdcage as just such a "made object": purposefully designed but not just utilitarian—birdcages tend to be fanciful creations, often quite beautiful. So the empty, discarded birdcage becomes, in your eye, an analogue for the unread poem? (This may be a total non sequitur, but when I finished writing this poem, I read it aloud to fellow poet Bruce Taylor, whose immediate response was, "I want that birdcage.") But "Castoffs" is about discarded things in general—not just intact ones— and what prompted it was not thoughts about the value of discarded things but thoughts about their poignancy, the peculiar sadness that seeing such things can evoke in us. The first stanza of the poem lists things once valued and used, discarded because they are broken or damaged. I contrast these with the "intact, discarded." It's sad to see a thing still potentially useful languish unused and unappreciated; it seems a waste. To me, the "perfectly good" birdcage is poignant because it suggests that the bird has died and the owner does not want the cage around as a sad reminder. Yet there's also, in the title of the poem, a hint that it isn't just the owner who has cast off the cage—it's the bird. A bird that lived its life caged. The cage is meaningless without the bird; every detail was designed for the bird—but birds weren't designed to live in cages.

"The Unharmed," a poem that stands out to me in your oeuvre, ends, "We are the writing that stayed dry, / and cannot read itself." Those of us unharmed by war have a responsibility, you suggest, but does the poem see us living up to that responsibility?

It's my own generation the poem invokes—the immediate postwar generation, whose parents were starting families in the optimism of that era, putting the war years behind them. We were their "message in a bottle" cast into the future, the embodiment of their hopes for a better world their generation fought for—but, being born when we were, we knew only the wake of the war, the subsiding waves that "rocked our cradle." With no personal memory of the war years, with only what we could glean second hand (and many of those who fought chose not to talk to their children about the war, or airbrushed what little they did share), we were largely innocent of the turmoil that preceded our arrival. For us, by and large, the war had already receded into history. The message of hope and renewal that our mere existence signified was lost on us.

Carmine Starnino has written about the centrality of the themes in your poem, "Bounty," from *A Day's Grace* (2003). You once joked with me you wished you'd never written it. Do you still feel that way?

Well, I was joking, but certain poems, for whatever reason, do receive disproportionate attention. I've had two poems follow me around that way. The first was "Maintenance"— written in 1981 and anthologized eight times in the next seven years, as though I'd never written anything else. It's an early poem, it isn't particularly representative of my poetry, and even if it were, it would not be the poem I'd personally choose to represent my poetry. In more recent years, "Bounty" (the poem you're referring to) has dogged me in a different way. One reviewer after another has singled it out, latching onto the line you quoted as a sum-up of my ars poetica—as if my personal aesthetic could be reduced to "small is beautiful." And I think this is misleading. While it's true my poems often give sustained attention to small, ordinary things—the kinds of things most people don't notice, or don't notice themselves noticing, or would never think of writing about—my motivation is not some literary version of affirmative action on behalf of small things. It isn't the smallness of a thing that prompts me to write about it, but rather what it evokes, the metaphoric resonances I sense in it. And these can be missed by someone looking only at *what* is being described in a poem and not at *how* it is being described. I can understand why someone writing about my work might find "Make much of something small" a convenient tag for generalizing about my poetry, but this not only misses the metaphysical aspect of my poetry (by which I mean the levels of metaphor or allegory beneath the surface of what some might take to be merely descriptive)—it ignores the context of that line in "Bounty," a December poem. The month of December is a time of diminishment: the light has dropped, the trees are bare, our days are largely housebound—we have to content ourselves with less. This is not saying "less is more"; it is talking about a *time* when we need to make more of less. I also think the poem's appeal—subliminally, at least—is based as much on its formal music (my use of unpatterned metre, rhyme, and refrain in regular stanzas) as on its meaning: the line resonates in the way that it does for musical reasons.

The speaker in "Brink" from *Pause for Breath* (2009) seems to prefer the "roaring" and "soaring" spaces of night over the "blank ache" of day. Is this preference just about night over day? Or does dream play a part?

"Brink" is about that pre-dawn state of half-waking when "words unpinned from their meanings" float through our heads—nonsensical phrases, vestiges of dreaming that made some sort of sense a moment or two ago but suddenly have lost their context. It's a state when we can either tumble back into sleep or come to full consciousness—that brief tussle between the unconscious and the conscious mind (it occurs to me that one of my early books was titled *The Space Between Sleep and Waking*). There is the dim awareness of what awaits if we allow consciousness to win: the daytime world with its "labyrinthine paths"—the forced march of its routines and responsibilities, its convoluted detours and dead ends. By contrast, the unconscious mind is unfettered; it can leap right over the rat paths we humans make for ourselves. There's always a reluctance to get up in the morning; we're tugged back towards sleep—the snooze button was invented to indulge this. But that in-between state is very hard to hold onto. I like to get to my desk very early in the morning and try to write a few words before daytime imperatives have had a chance to intrude on it. To bring my "bed head" to the desk.

Do you have a set time for writing? Daily? Or is it less organized for you?

It depends—what you mean by writing. I keep a journal (not daily—and lately I find myself writing in it much less frequently than I used to), and I maintain lengthy correspondences, now largely in the form of email. Or I may be chipping away at some piece of solicited or commissioned literary journalism—but I don't think of any of this as my "real" writing. That begins in something called my "Daily Notebooks"—the name is a joke, because I often go weeks or months without writing in them. But when I'm in a phase of using them, I do write in them daily—not a lot; I sit at it for an hour or so, usually before breakfast—yielding anywhere from a few lines about the weather or the view out the window to a few pages of free association—largely illegible to anybody but me, and sometimes even to me (more than one serendipitous poem owes its inspiration to a misreading of my own handwriting). I date the entries and look back over them frequently, searching for lines or phrases that might have potential, something I can carry forward to a fresh page and play around with. Most of my poems have had their beginnings in these notebooks, and some of my short stories (essays I usually compose directly on computer). Sometimes I finish a poem the same day or the next day, but more usually, they grow slowly, over several sessions—sometimes on consecutive days, sometimes spread over weeks or months, even years. When I'm convinced I've got something worth finishing, I move a working draft onto the computer (as I used to move it onto my manual typewriter) and continue by printing out, inking over, and retyping successive drafts. Once I am actively working on something, the writing sessions get longer—anywhere from two or three hours to most of the day—but they aren't necessarily daily. And I tend to have more than one piece of writing in the works at any given time, moving back and forth between projects. Things often take a long time to finish, or get shelved for long periods. I'm not sure this qualifies as a routine—at least, not in the usual sense of the word—but periodic attempts to be more organized about it have never lasted very long.

Do you think of yourself as an experimenter? That has complicated connotations, but the introduction to your book *Digressions: Prose Poems, Collage Poems, and Sketches* (2012) seems to imply it, with its emphasis on "variety" and "variation"—especially as regards the collage poems.

No, I don't think of myself as an experimenter—not in the sense of pushing the boundaries of poetry in any original way. Prose poems are nothing new, and poets have been fooling around with found material and collaged phrases at least since the 1960s. If anything, most critics peg me as a traditionalist. Yet I like to try different things, and I believe that, on some level, *every* poem is an experiment. For me, the impulse towards a poem sparks a negotiation between the thing I'm casting to say and the structure that will best allow me to say it. (I use the word "casting" here because I rarely know what it is I want to say before I have found the structure to say it in—so there is a simultaneous feeling around for both, and each begins to define the other as the poem finds its voice.) It's important to me that each poem be allowed to find its own voice and shape. It is *not* important to me that my collections have a uniform tone or a uniform look on the page—which is why, before I collected the prose poems in *Digressions*, they were scattered through my previous collections, among the free verse and formal poems that are my more usual mode. My penchant for variation is not something I impose on my poems out of a doctrinaire belief in variety for its own sake; it's something that happens naturally because I respect each poem's right to evolve in its own time and its own way—and also because I get restless working in any one mode for any length of time.

Yet "Gleanings at Year's End" pushes at the boundaries of being a sonnet, no? Do you think labels such as "traditionalist" or "experimenter" are useful? Or problematic?

Writing in forms has always been one option for me. I have no axe to grind either for or against tradition, for or against experimentation. I can't remember if I was even aware that "Gleanings at Year's End" was a fourteen-line poem; I was not trying to write a sonnet. But in one of my early books, *Becoming Light* (1987), I did consciously experiment with, or edge back towards, sonnet form: that collection includes a number of fourteen-line poems in which I played with different aspects of the sonnet. I say "edge back" because when we learned about the form in high school and university, I found I could easily write strict classical sonnets—not necessarily inspired poems but perfect exemplars. So I had sonnet basics in my head early on—not just the rhyme/ metre requirements but the rhetorical framing, whether on the Petrarchan octave-sestet paradigm or the Shakespearean three-quatrains-and-a-couplet one. These compositional principles influenced some early poems of mine that were not sonnets but borrowed some formal features of them. At twenty-three, I wrote one quite classical sonnet, with a mix of Petrarchan and Elizabethan features and an untraditional rhyme scheme, that I never bothered to submit for publication because this was a time when Canadian literary magazines wouldn't touch a rhyming, metred poem with a stick. "Blowing the Fluff Away" resurfaced more than thirty years later; it was published in *Poetry* in 2009, and I included it in *Pause for Breath* the same year. The whole "traditional" vs. "experimental" thing is really so much about fashion—which brings me back to those sonnet-like poems in *Becoming Light*. By that time—in the mid-1980s—a number of poets were experimenting with what they called sonnets. There were those who claimed that *any* fourteen-line poem could be called a sonnet, and that if you wrote fourteen lines in free verse, you were pushing the boundaries of the sonnet. I thought this was nonsense; there's more to a sonnet than line count. My own experiments involved configuring the argument in different line groupings, instead of the traditional 8-6 or 4-4-4-2. I tried 7-7 and 10-4 (with and without stanza break); I tried a block of twelve short lines in free verse followed by a traditional Shakespearean closing couplet, end-rhymed in iambic pentameter; I played around with unpatterned rhyme and internal rhyme, untraditional metres and no metre. I didn't really consider these poems sonnets. They were more like a salute to sonnets. Later, when form poetry was starting to regain respectability, I wrote the occasional classical sonnet in contemporary language and a few truly boundary-pushing ones (see "To a Daughter in her Twentieth Year" and "Salve" in *A Day's Grace*).

You end "A Guide to Modern Verse" with the phrase "sheer insistence." Does a poet have to insist these days on being read?

The "sheer insistence" I was referring to is the force of repetition on the mind of a reader—not the forcing of the poet's will on a readership. Many people have a fear of modern poetry because they think they won't "get it". I meant to suggest that familiarizing oneself with the words, "closing the distance / that made them strange," can be enough for us to appreciate a poem even if we don't understand it. (I savour any number of poems by Wallace Stevens, among others, that I cannot pretend to understand but can recite with gusto.) The three last lines, "The way a name / grows onto a baby, / from sheer insistence," allude to how, at first, it feels strange to attach a name to a little baby; it's only by repetition, the insistent application of the label—using it ourselves and hearing others use it—that the name begins to stick. In the same way, we may come to savour a strange or difficult poem just by reading it enough times, allowing it to "grow on us."

The title poem in your new collection is full of media: television, radio, dreamy films, and subtitles. (The line "Where is my toboggan" makes me think of Orson Welles's "Rosebud.") The poem's major refrain is "It was the beginning of dwindle." But there seems to be hope, growth (even pleasure?). Do these media play a part in that?

Media are not the focus of this poem. Yes, there's a description of a movie, but it is really more vision than movie—something playing behind my own eyelids, with a soundtrack of leaves rustling. Welles's "Rosebud" was nowhere in my mind when I alluded to the toboggan. Yes, a television set makes a cameo appearance—but only as a sort of shrine on which family artifacts are displayed.

The radio is mentioned only as the source of an old advertising jingle and of the CBC's time signal—capping a list of other sounds, many long obsolete, that were once part of the aural landscape of daily life. The pleasures invoked in the poem (and I'm glad you recognized there is hope, growth, and pleasure in this poem!) have nothing to do with media. They are remembered pleasures of childhood (trampoline, toboggan, monkey bars, roller skates, swings, jumping downstairs)—outdoor activities, all of them associated with moments when the feet are not in contact with the ground, moments of defying gravity. The connection here is to the theme of shoes, foreshadowed in the poem's title but not introduced until the bronzed baby shoes appear in the sixth movement of the poem: "first of the outgrown shoes," preserved as a sentimental keepsake. Our existence as humans with feet on the ground, as opposed to babes in arms, begins with putting on shoes: we walk the earth in shoes. From here on in the poem, shoes reappear in different life contexts. As I'm sure is obvious, "the beginning of dwindle" refers to a time of life—the dawning awareness that one's prime years are over—in a poem that alludes again and again to the end of summer. But a contrapuntal energy comes from those vivid memories of childhood threaded through it as the poem works its way to an acceptance of the present. I think this poem is as much celebration as elegy.

But how can one read about childhood and a toboggan—not to mention movies—and not think of *Citizen Kane*? That is, even if unintentional, the resonance is there. Is that a problem, you think?

No, why should it be? Readers naturally bring their own associations to a poem and may hear resonances that the poet either did not intend at all or did not intend consciously. Of course, "How can one … not think of *Citizen Kane*?" begs the question of whether one has seen the movie and whether one needs to have seen it to respond to the toboggan in my poem. I did see *Citizen Kane*, but it didn't make much of an impression on me. But if I say Rosebud was not in my head when I wrote "Where is my toboggan?", it doesn't mean it can't be in yours when you read it. "What a poem means" doesn't stop at "what the poet meant." Still, I think any reading of a poem should first pay close attention to the context of the relevant words, lines, or phrases within the poem itself, to give the poet's intentions a fair shake.

"Shoes" and "doctors" come up a few times in the new book, not least in "It Is Not in Great Acts." Would you agree that it's a poem that has little patience for the heroic in poetry, anti-Romantic and free of irony as it is?

Ah, "free of irony"—that has become a sin, hasn't it? Odd you would single out this poem, which a recent reviewer excoriated for its banality. You could say it's a poem *about* banality, if that is what you want to call people's modest desires even while they imagine themselves meant for greater things. In a collection whose focus is largely on "time past," I felt there should be a poem about "time present," and this one, with its summer imagery, seemed a good fit, though it predates the rest of the book by many years.

It's also stylistically atypical of my work. It was written as a theme poem for the Festival franco-anglais de poésie in Paris, a translation festival whose theme that year (2005) was "Reality Dreams." (I almost never begin a poem with a subject, so my contribution evolved from already-existing bits and pieces that loosely fit the theme.) The fact that the poem was created in order to be translated into French, to a deadline, influenced my linguistic choices: the vocabulary is straightforward, the line breaks reflect syntactical units, I avoided tricky enjambments and the kinds of compression and wordplay that are more characteristic of my poetry, because I knew the difficulties these pose for translators. This may make the poem less satisfying to sophisticated readers, but I think it has something to say that doesn't often get said—namely, that the "great acts" of war and revolution have as their ultimate goal the restoration of a world in which people's basic needs and modest aspirations, banal though they may seem, are not denied.

In Which the Journey Is a Dream

A.F. MORITZ

Albert Frank Moritz was born in Niles, Ohio, in 1947 and educated at Marquette University in Wisconsin, where he completed a PhD in British poetry (1700–1900) in 1975. He has published twenty books of poetry, translations from the French (Benjamin Péret) and Spanish (Ludwig Zeller), and nonfiction with his wife Theresa (biographies of Stephen Leacock and Emma Goldman). Among his many honours, he has received an Ingram Merrill Foundation Fellowship (1982) and a Guggenheim Fellowship (1990). Three times a finalist for the Governor General's Literary Award for Poetry (2000, 2008, 2012), he was awarded the Griffin Prize for Poetry for *The Sentinel* in 2009. At the time of the interview, he had just published *Sequence* (2015). *The Sparrow: Selected Poems* appeared in 2018 and *As Far As You Know* in 2020. This interview was begun in September 2015. Moritz lives in Toronto.

I'd like to start back some—with your decision to leave the US. You're not a draft dodger. Can you tell me about your move to Canada?

Theresa and I and our son Blaise, then three years old, came to Toronto so that Theresa could enter the doctoral program in medieval studies at the University of Toronto. This was in September of 1974. While I had been doing my doctorate at Marquette University, 1970 to 1974, in eighteenth- and nineteenth-century British poetry, she marked time getting master's degrees in Spanish and in English and, in the latter, became fascinated by aspects of the Middle Ages, and she even had written a book on the ordering of *The Canterbury Tales*, published by the Ohio State University Press. She was a brilliant student, could have gone to various high prestige places, but Toronto was recommended as the very best and, in addition, the city was a media centre. So maybe I could help support us through journalism, in which I had a degree and considerable work experience. And it was a literary hub, which interested us greatly.

Another factor for me was that I was happy to be going into voluntary exile for political reasons. The election of 1972—in which the excellent George McGovern was trounced by Richard Nixon even though it was known to a moral certainty that Nixon was guilty of the things for which he was later impeached and resigned—convinced me that "the great American public" knew and cared nothing for the Constitution, American traditions, the essence of America as found in Thoreau and Whitman and Emerson and Melville, cared in fact only for the representation and continuance of the immediate status quo ante in terms of class, power, wealth, and publicity. In other words, "conservatism" in the sense of inertia. I don't like a principled conservatism, but I don't scorn it and I don't think it is impossible. There's no such thing, however, to be found in America.

Can we discuss "Kissinger at the Funeral of Nixon" in this biographical light?

When Nixon died in 1994, I sat watching parts of his protracted funeral, the various ceremonials in Washington, and then the helicopter delivery of his body to California. I listened to Henry Kissinger's eulogy. And I heard and read a lot of commentary on his career. A lot of it, whatever stripe of opinion it emanated from, was good: informed, alert, insightful. And yet it didn't tell me anything I didn't know, and I thought it missed the essence. I thought: I can do better than that, and the reason is that the truth about Nixon is one of those many absolutely central, utterly essential things that can only be put in poetry … the fact that few read poetry, or have the ability to read it anymore, explains a good deal of why society is in increasingly parlous shape for lack of the basic nutriments of human sensibility.

It's a dramatic monologue, but it's really interior discourse à la Virginia Woolf. Kissinger is portrayed as thinking a long skein of thoughts to himself as, adeptly but distractedly, he mouths the funeral oration that he actually gave. In this interior monologue, he even refers to some of the things he is saying (that is, did say) out loud, to the assembled. The myth of the poem then is the idea of conscience, that Kissinger, my Kissinger, represents someone who knows perfectly well that the things he does and says have a different motive, meaning, and goal from the one he bruits. This characterization of Kissinger's mind is paralleled and buttressed by an aspect of his reflection on Nixon: that Nixon was the founder of one of the basic elements of current "culture"—namely, the behaviour of resolutely affirming whatever foolish or criminal thing one has done and gathering, if one can, a party around it. I'd identify that as Kissinger's dream-nightmare, that he is suddenly Ahab's mate. Unfortunately, it may belong only to my Kissinger, not to Kissinger. But peace. Who knows what may come to him?

Along these same lines, I've been thinking a lot about "Artisan and Clerk," with its focus on a better America. Is there a connection between that poem and Donald Trump's "Make America Great Again"?

I think to myself, "Great again compared to when?" On the question of economic prosperity, everyone wants the great American market, but if businesses continue to move elsewhere, pay lower wages, put downward pressure on benefits and lifestyle, there soon won't be any great American market. This is exactly like trying to convince termites not to eat the house they're living in. "Artisan and Clerk" is about the profundity of that problem, not anything Trump can grasp.

The illusionistic nostalgia, and the element of coded racism, in Trump's "Make America Great Again" is almost the least of the potential evils the slogan expresses. Most politicians are blind to the fact that they only serve, and only can serve, the basic drift of our world. As Jacques Ellul says, we have to recognize that there is good politics and bad politics and we have to support the good with all our strength, as if it really mattered, but in the current situation, politics is completely helpless. True power is elsewhere. The politician who did anything about technology and economic power except work to augment them for the competitive benefit of his country (while mouthing the empty "ideas" that, oh no, competition isn't a cut-throat game to dominate and eliminate, it's good for everyone!) would be out of office immediately. You can "lead" a great corporation as long as you lead it to make more money, cover more territory, destroy more rivals. You can be a "visionary" of the future, like Steve Jobs, as long as your visions and your future are to make more powerful, faster, universal versions of exactly what we've got and what we're doing. The great horror of Trump is that he is not even, as a politician, someone who is consciously or unconsciously a helpless servant of the drift. He's one of its partisans, one of its enthusiastic helpers, one for whom criticism of it means only criticizing whatever holds it back from growing still more omnipresent and dominant.

Let's step back a bit: What was literary Toronto like when you arrived?

By the spring of 1975, I had my feet under me enough to go out and try to make some acquaintances in poetry. I have to record with gratitude that perhaps the first thing I did was go up to York University, on a very wintry, windy day—and to go to York in bad weather in those days was like going to the moon—to hear a poetry reading by Giorgio Di Cicco, whom I'd read about as one of the most prominent and promising of the new poets. He read excellently and made a lot of humour out of a mouse that ran up the tall curtain on a window behind him as he read one poem, and he befriended me as soon as I talked with him.

Around this time, a great Toronto tradition called the Bohemian Embassy moved from its long-standing place to a room in the just-then-developing Harbourfront Centre, and this reading series was run by Greg Gatenby. I would go there practically every Tuesday and hear the readings, and sometimes give one.

I believe I experienced the tag end of one of the great times for poetry in Toronto. One result of this activity was that an international poetry conference was organized and held at Hart House. I was lucky to be selected one of ten younger poets who got to read in panels and on the stage with international invitees. As a result, I met Yehuda Amichai, for instance. This poetry conference of several days, with an impressive international roster, was the ultimate origin of today's International Festival of Authors. Greg Gatenby established it as a rather modest yearly festival surrounding his weekly series of readings and still mainly devoted to poetry. Over the years, it grew and finally has almost entirely deleted poetry, without which it wouldn't exist. Kind of like the rest of the world. At this festival in its earlier years, I heard and got to shake hands with Octavio Paz.

There was always a sense of your writing being outside what was happening in Canada, and yet what you describe sounds much more friendly and approachable. Is this a myth of the times?

Maybe like me, you sometimes think back to your childhood and wonder whether it was happy or miserable, convivial or lonely. Truth is, probably, it was both. I'd say the same about my poetry childhood in Canada. I was indeed off to one side, but for the first five years or so, I was so intent on my own work, primarily, but also on the people I knew in poetry, and some of the activity of trying to get published, that it took up my attention. One is happy in activity. I ran into some opposition and some bad luck in getting my books published, and three quarters of the work I had finished in my twenties did not appear until the early '80s. This was a barrier, obviously, to anyone's recognizing what my work *was*. Then, I got sick of advertising, which was my livelihood, and Theresa and I decided to make a living as independent authors of books, nonfiction. We wrote some good books, but as a living, it was not one. We got poorer and poorer. In 1980 or '81, a combination of poverty and the extreme, energy-draining busyness that it always entails in anyone who hasn't simply given up made me unable to participate in literary society anymore, and this lasted for twelve, thirteen years: 1980 to 1992, inclusive. I'd say I was completely isolated during this stretch.

You also wrote some early reviews which separated you from the in crowd.

It's possibly true that I occasioned some of my isolation and my feeling of disaffection through my reviewing. In 1977 through 1979, I was the chief reviewer for poetry for the old *Books in Canada* under the editorship of Doug Marshall. During this period, I did twenty-nine reviews for the magazine. I enjoyed and am proud of a lot of this activity. My bio-critical article on Miriam Waddington is still, to the shame of the academy, cited as the most extensive piece of writing on her work. I welcomed Margaret Avison's *Sunblue*, from a tiny Nova Scotia press, in very round and vivid terms when it had otherwise gone unnoticed and when awareness of Avison was in a trough. I reviewed with high praise Erin Moure's first book, from galleys, before it was published, and the review influenced, I would say even determined, the terms in which that book and her next two were discussed.

On the other hand, I savaged some poets who were much more prominent and influential than these, dismissing books of theirs that everyone else approved and which are now generally regarded as classics. This didn't win me any affection, I imagine. But as I said before, there were other reasons for my disappearance and isolation, having to do simply with hard times.

I'd like to move now to your latest book, *Sequence*. Am I right to think that this book comes out of an occasion which isn't discussed in the text?

I had (or have?) aortal stenosis. This is an arterial hardening, and what it does is progressively narrow the degree to which the aortal valve opens, until a crisis state is reached, at which point the valve needs to be replaced, now that it can be replaced. This is a congenital condition. It was diagnosed in me as the condition underlying a heart murmur that emerged in one of my yearly physical exams in my early fifties. The cardiologist told me that the condition generally bespeaks itself in the fifties and has to be corrected in the sixties. This is exactly what happened with me. I'd been under observation for it for thirteen years when Dr. Drobac (Milutin Drobac) said to me he was sending me to his surgeon, Dr. David (Tirone David) for his opinion.

While all this was happening, I was struggling to complete my book. After the operation—this is a serious procedure, and it was difficult, and I had some complications, was in the hospital longer than had been expected—I wasn't up to much. Strength only gradually returned, and then only a little of it. It may be that this experience intensified the book. The whole situation and how I handled it certainly seems to parallel the themes.

I was going to dedicate the book to Theresa. I always think this is a sort of imposture. I could dedicate a book to many people, but not to her, because to dedicate it to her belittles her importance to it, which is total. As if I could really offer it to her in any way that goes beyond the way she has first offered it. Really, it ought to be she who dedicates my own book to me. But I thought of dedicating this one to her, but she said no, dedicate it to the doctors, and that's what we did.

In the note to Part III, you write, "The details of this section are from my experience, but…" There are clearly fictional and biographical elements to the "I," who at one point says, "I am more than eighty years old…" Is the "I" consistent throughout? Or should we identify the "I" differently in each of the ten parts of the poem?

Identity is a vexed question. The book's meant to convey in its very form my feeling that in all its variety and changes, identity *is* identity, identity does exist, and does so through dedication, through unity of effort: "What thou lov'st well shall not be reft from thee / What thou lov'st well is thy true heritage." A person is a vow, a promise he makes to himself and others, a faithfulness to a love, and not in the sense that we usually give to making a vow but in the sense of a decision which is an orientation of the total self. This grows from the self's origin, develops and increases, and gradually reveals its form and becomes apparent. Hence the importance of the theme of "roots." Our first place seems to be our first love, first loyalty, or at least to express our first love well, to symbolize it well. At the same time, we have to move—we're not rooted; if we don't move, we won't be living and human—so as to be or become worthy of the one we love. As Jiménez says: "Roots and wings. But let the wings take root, and the roots fly."

But *Sequence* is also a story.

I might discuss its story as one would discuss a novel. If you could go to the Greece of the time of *Zorba the*

Greek, you would expect not to find Zorba. Zorba and the whole foreground of the novel is created by the novelist for his expressive purposes. On the other hand, you would expect to find the landscape, the material culture of the small towns, the folkways, exactly as Kazantzakis describes them, and you wouldn't be disappointed, no doubt. These are exactly true. On the other hand, in the foreground story, there are also many incidents, personal characteristics, and other elements that occurred in life— whether in Kazantzakis's own life or in lives he knows about—and that have been adapted into the fiction and that might be discovered. At this point, the truth of the foreground story and the truth of the background story blend their different natures. It's like this with my poem.

What about the form?

An idea, a feeling, found often in the book is that each day is a life, and so is each breath, each step, if we could only feel it: step, breath, day, life are equivalents, just as Gabriel Marcel shows us that life, hope, and creativity are equivalents. We struggle to affirm the automatic ongoingness of the body—breath—which can be a torture to us when we would like to leave life but our animal won't let us. We struggle to connect the breath to the step, the willed going forward, the work we accept in one way or another, though it too can become just a weariness, a torture. These things have a rhythm. They mean that something stops and starts that does not stop and start, but continues, flows. The heart pulses and the breath moves like a goldfinch, which beats its wings and rises and then folds them and dips and then beats them again and rises, making a path of plateaus and shallow valleys.

I am trying to make the "free" verse itself a symbol—that is, an emblem that is an emblem because it is another thing belonging to the same genus—of the flight of the bird. Each line is a segment of flight separate from and connected to the others, with mysterious gaps or cessations, which are not gaps or cessations, in between.

I feel this is a meaning inherent in free verse and, in another way, in verse itself. More regular verse seems to mean the relatively trustworthy stability of repetition in similar form, yet the danger and questioning of the stops and turns are there. Free verse seems to emphasize the difficult need to remake each increment as a new thing, a new beginning, that is yet similar to the past it's part of. It needs to make itself as a corresponding, if very different, component, independent yet dependent, apart yet part, in order that the being should not disintegrate. It also seems to emphasize willy-nilly the sense of threat that exists in pulse, breath, and step—that each might be the last, that the heart might not start up again, that the most recent footfall might prove the final one.

There are a number of refrains in *Sequence*, not least "What did you come out into the desert to see?" This is biblical and, like Jesus, the speaker refers to himself as a "wanderer." Where is the modern world in the poem?

As perhaps doesn't need to be said after our comments about "Kissinger at the Funeral of Nixon" and "Artisan and

Clerk," the modern and contemporary world is all over my poems—in its material reality, in its conditions and themes, in its politics and sociology, in its incidents and personalities. I think of myself as the unity of my tensions, a unity forever sought, and one of my chief tensions is: Should I be Whitman or should I be Mallarmé? Should I include everything explicitly—which is so beautiful a thing to do, so powerful, so right—or should I severely essentialize, going deep, deep to the very end of depth, through one tiny jewel of approach, making as little concession as possible to any verbal elements other than the strictest needs of refined poetic expression—which is so beautiful a thing to do?

Sequence represents a moment of reaction from Whitman toward Mallarmé. I said to myself I wanted to sink, if that's the word, into spiritual basics and for once leave the specificity of the moment and history, our wars and our poisoning of the earth, etc., outside my door. In this sense, you might say that *Sequence* takes place, all of it, in a single day: the days, pages, breaths, steps, each of which make up a part of a life and yet also are a life entire. *Sequence*, the whole of it, might be all one breath, one step, in which, nevertheless, everything occurs and has occurred.

Part VI of *Sequence* begins, "Still another retelling of the tale from a minor player's part." It seems to me that *Sequence* both criticizes and works with that idea.

The idea of retelling a tale from the viewpoint of previously non-central characters goes way back. We only have to think of, for instance, *The Trojan Women*. Or Aeneas, previously a bit player, telling the tale of the fall of Troy … within whose re-envisioning is enfolded Sinon, previously it seems a non-existent player, telling the tale of the Greeks' apparent withdrawal. In our time, it would be hard to count the number of poetic inhabitings of Persephone, Eurydice, and so forth, sometimes to critique what tradition supposedly uses the stories to mean by telling them from an objective or an Orpheus-centred viewpoint, and sometimes to draw out meanings that tradition has supposedly missed. This has been a procedure for some of the greatest passages or poetic elements in some of the greatest recent poets. The poem-section of *Sequence* that you mention refers to Seferis, the crucial prominence of Elpenor in his versions of the voyage of Ulysses.

If you want to call the above sort of thinking criticism, then *Sequence*, and my work in general, criticizes the minor-character-narration sub-genre. Here, though, I think the important thing is to look at the meaning through the dramatic situation, not just the lyrical impression. It is Ulysses who laughs at the notion, not me. And then Ulysses turns out to be, or turns into, an incoherent homeless person. Reliable? The self who is harangued, sort of like the wedding guest in *The Rime of the Ancient Mariner*, has to contemplate the spectacle of a ruined person, whose eloquent existence emerges also (at least as symbolized in the poem) as pointed speech: a person who is emblematic but who completes being and acts with the word. It's the word, which comes only at the beginning, the first line and a half, that allows the speaker of the poem, the one confronted by "Ulysses," to see the reality. And near the end, he asks the question: "if we're not all kings, / we're nothing?"

Can you tell me something about the process of writing a longer piece like *Sequence*? Is it assembled sequentially? Or have the parts been moved around?

The answer is both. I had the idea of it, and this came after some of the poem-sections had been written as short poems—a page or usually less, sometimes much less. I thought these would make a succinct sequential poem, and as I began to assemble this, the idea for a more comprehensive book arose. This partially came as a concept and partially as a result of the continuing production of these short poems out of one another, as the existing ones provoked others and they seemed to strive to fill out an entire trajectory.

They also revivified and absorbed some previous material. For instance, the first six pages of Part VI, the pages about Ulysses that you mentioned in asking me the "minor character" question, were an earlier meditative poem. Some new material arose, and the existing material changed somewhat as this pre-existing poem separated into semi-independent poem-sections to fit into the concept of the forming book. A bigger example is Part III, the quasi-autobiographical part with the plot based very loosely on a one-paragraph incident in *Jude the Obscure*. This was something I intended to write and started to write about 1979 as a narrative poem on the models of "Aylmer's Field" and the early narratives of Robinson Jeffers's *Tamar* and "Roan Stallion," etc. I was going to write such a poem in an industrial context, not the context of the rural or the near-wilderness. Or, rather, the encroachment of the industrial on the rural and wilderness, which is the story of modernity. This project stalled, but there was a lot of existing material, and the love of the idea always stayed in my mind. One thing about poetry is that you're a poet entirely apart from writing anything because of the poems in your mind that as yet haven't gone farther.

God-Culture

ROBERT BRINGHURST

Robert Bringhurst was born in Los Angeles in 1946 and raised in western North America, moving back and forth across the US–Canada border. He moved to Vancouver in 1972 as a graduate student at the University of British Columbia and has lived on the BC coast ever since. He is the author of fourteen collections of poems, as well as pamphlets and broadsides, first collected in *The Beauty of the Weapons: Selected Poems 1972–1982* (1982). His *Selected Poems* was published in 2010. His manual *The Elements of Typographic Style*, first published in 1993, has been translated into ten languages and is a standard in the field. His three-volume *Masterworks of the Classical Haida Mythtellers* was enthusiastically reviewed in the *Times* of London by Margaret Atwood and chosen as the *Times* Literary Editor's Book of the Year in 2004. A new edition of volume one of that trilogy was published in London by the Folio Society in 2015. His recent books include *Going Down Singing* (2016), *Ten Poems with One Title* (2022) and *The Ridge* (2023). This interview was begun in February 2017. Bringhurst lives on Quadra Island, BC.

Can I begin by asking about form? Do rhyme and meter hold any interest for you?

As a kid, I messed around with whatever came my way—music, painting, poetry, carpentry, auto mechanics, and so on—but the first art in which I had any formal instruction was architecture. In architecture, form is not optional. You can vary it, of course. You can also disguise it, masking the real structure with a decorative surface, but if you leave it out or get it wrong, your building collapses. It's not much different in carpentry or mechanics. That's the kind of form that interests me: the kind without which your engine doesn't run and your sonata doesn't either.

Then, of course, there's beauty. Not as something painted on but as liveliness and grace intrinsic to the structure. A good building doesn't just accommodate people's needs. It doesn't just give them adequate headroom and a place to go to the toilet. It improves the rhythm and texture of life for the people inside it—and for those outside it too. I want that kind of literary structure. It doesn't come from mindlessly repeated pilasters or quatrains, but it also doesn't come from simply turning on the garden hose of language.

Good carpenters get interested in wood. They stop thinking of it as board feet of lumber and start to see it as tissue—living tissue whose life has been arrested and whose form has been, for a while at least, preserved. They start to collaborate with the wood instead of simply sawing it up and nailing it back together. That's how I try to work with wood myself, and that's the way I like to work with language. Few things interest me less than regular picket fences or purely formalist verse, but sensual and intellectual pleasure both interest me a lot. A good piece of carpentry makes you want to reach out and touch it. A good piece of writing makes you want to say the words aloud, to feel them in your mouth and in your mind. That's not everything in life, but it's a part of what I'm after.

Rhyme and meter are natural features of language. But of course, in natural speech, the rhymes are mostly imperfect, and they occur at irregular intervals. And in natural speech, the meter keeps varying too, like the grain of wood or the texture of a forest. That's the kind of rhyme and meter that appeals to me most. The enchanted forest is really a forest; it isn't an orchard.

In the introduction to your 1982 selected poems, you write, "Most of the poems are products more of oral composition than of writing." How does the oral composition work with visual poetry effects—for instance, enjambment?

When I'm writing down a poem, I choose the line ends and stanza breaks as carefully as I do the words—but if the whole spatial arrangement disappeared, I wouldn't lose a lot of sleep over it. Either the typographic form is real—which is to say, you can hear it in the language, so you or someone else could reconstruct it if you lost it—or else it doesn't matter very much.

Poetry, as you know, is a whole lot older than writing. When European scribes began transcribing the poems they heard, or poems they'd composed, they wrote them down the same way they wrote everything else: with no spaces between the words and no breaks between the lines or stanzas. The line breaks in Homer and Aeschylus, Sappho and Sophocles, were put there centuries later by editors— and the editors could do this because the lines, like the words, were audible. The poems are metrical, which makes this process easy most of the time, but not always. The meter of the choral odes of Aeschylus and Pindar, Sophocles and Euripides, is generally complex. So editors disagree to some extent on how they should be written out or printed.

It's pretty much the same story elsewhere—in China, Egypt, Mesopotamia, and with Mayan scribes in Central America—except that there the editorial stage, when empty space was affordable, came later or never came at all. Even in Europe, the transition was much slower than you might suppose. In the sixteenth century, there were still writers and printers—including some very good writers and printers—who envisioned the prose book as a single 300-page paragraph.

We live in a time when paper is cheap—way cheaper than it ought to be—and typography is not just possible but universally available. I see this as a luxury—a really astonishing and unsustainable luxury, like air travel. Air travel, cheap paper, and good type are available to me now, so I do what I can with them. But the best mode of travel, so far as I'm concerned, is walking, not flying or driving a car. And the best way of taking in a poem is to speak it or hear it spoken aloud. If the arrangement of words on the page helps you speak the poem or hear it, then it's useful, but like the airplane, the ferry, or the car, the page is an intermediate conveyance: a way of getting quickly from one listening place or thinking place to another.

You've been very quietly revising your poems over the years. "Bone Flute Breathing," between your 1982 selected poems and the more recent 2009 ones, for instance, has some subtle differences. Do the changes reflect the oral composition? Or are they editorial?

Any poem that stays in my active repertoire, or returns to it after an absence, is in danger of revision. If I don't perform it, nothing is likely to happen to it. If I do perform it, some words might change or some lines might drop out or get added. By this time, however, I'm working with and on a written text. The process is oral, but it hardly qualifies as oral composition. If you want a name for it, you could call it oral editing. It's oral because, once a poem is written down, I tend to hear it more closely if I perform it than if I read it sotto voce to myself or stare in silence at a printed version.

The fact is, I write and edit everything aloud—prose as well as poetry. I've done this with poetry for as long as I can remember. And until I started doing it with prose, my prose was pretty dreadful.

What do you see as the difference between prose and poetry, if the visual aspect is less significant?

Texture. There's more of it in poetry, less of it in prose. And it seems to me this is not just a matter of language.

A poem has something to say, and the thing it has to say reverberates or resonates with the rest of reality in a way that is not prosaic. Even before it's written, a poem is in motion, and its motion has a texture. It doesn't just walk or stride or shuffle along; it dances.

But once it's composed, a poem, like a piece of prose, becomes a structure of words, not just a fistful of rhythms or a tissue of unarticulated ideas. We expect, in that structure of words, some perceptible reflection or refraction of the resonance or texture of the subject of the poem: some echo of the texture that was there before the words.

If the texture we're offered in the finished work is purely visual—just an artful arrangement of words on the page—then I think it's a cheat. It could disappear for good through someone's stripping out the tabs and hard returns. If that's the case, then the texture you see is not in the language, it's just in the typing. The poem, if it is a poem, has something resonant to say and needs to resonantly say it. The something-to-say and the saying itself will fuse if things go well. If that happens, there'll be something you can hear as well as think: a phonological texture, a semiotic texture, and a syntactical texture too. There will be prosody, in other words—and a three-stranded prosody at that: texture of sound, texture of meaning, texture of grammar. If you live in a literate culture, you can represent at least some of this prosody visually. And if *that* visual representation were lost, it could be decently restored by re-transcribing the spoken words.

What about the historical connection between truth and poetry?

Goethe, as you know, wrote a book called *Poetry and Truth*, and it purports to be historical as well as personal. But I don't think poetry and truth are what *Dichtung und Wahrheit* is actually about.

We can learn quite a bit about poetry and truth if we skip Goethe's love affair with himself and read his poetry instead—but then what we learn isn't historical, it's ontological. That's probably where we should start. Poetry is a property of reality. So is truth. If we try to approach them historically, what we're mostly going to get is the history of *us*: the history of the ways in which we've mangled and misunderstood them, even at times tried pitting them against each other.

In most oral societies, literature is the major art form, and the main genre in oral literature isn't the novel, it's mythtelling. Myths are conveyed through narrative poetry. So in oral cultures, by and large, poetry is the main way of trying to tell the truth. That, in a nutshell, is the history of poetry and truth for the first nine-tenths of human existence. Then you start to get literacy. Then pretty soon you get prose and mathematics. You start to get experimental science. You get historical, philosophical, epistolary, and scientific writing. Later still, you get prose fiction. Now you have lots of ways of trying to tell the truth—and lots of ways of trying not to—so different truths get told. A lot of humans get more interested in themselves than they are in the larger world. This isn't just a literary phenomenon, of course. Urbanization, central heating, fossil fuel, and the electrical grid have a lot to do with it too. Print and broadcast journalism accelerate it. The internet sets it ablaze. People find themselves living in a sea of human voices, most of them talking of small-time human concerns. Human truth—heavily laced with human falsehood—obscures all other truth, and poetry suffers, like everything else, in these conditions.

Can I ask about your process of composition for a poem? How does the writing of one of your poems begin and end?

Those are the parts of the process I know least about, so there's not much I can tell you. I become aware of the poem first when some part of it comes into view: a verbal phrase, or a rhythmical shape, or a little melody, or just a sense of connection between some ideas. Where did it come from and how long was it under my tongue or behind that tree before I was aware of it? I have no idea.

The other end of the process is equally elusive. At some point, I've seen what I can see, done what I can do, and any attempt to do more will be counterproductive. So it's a lot like watching birds. If the venture is successful, the end product isn't a bird in a cage, nor a mounted specimen, nor dinner. The end product is spiritual and intellectual nourishment. Part of which lies in knowing that the bird escaped—frightened perhaps but unharmed and, if I'm *really* lucky, nourished in its turn.

Another thing I can say is that this beginning and ending is happening all the time. In that respect, again, it's a lot like watching animals. I live, as you know, in a house in the forest. I walk in the forest every day. I see many of the same individuals and species day after day, year after year. I learn a little more about them with every encounter. The poems I write down are the poems that reveal themselves to me in a similar way: an occasional major revelation but mostly a little bit here, a little bit there. A few lines a day if I'm lucky. I never get close to knowing all that could be known about the other creatures living here—and I never know all there is to know about the poems I'm writing down. So the text I can read to an audience or give to a publisher is always provisional.

How do you approach the translation of literature? Does the bird metaphor you used above extend to translation? That is, can your translation nourish the original? Is that desirable?

That's a lovely idea. I suppose, in a perfect world, it would be true. Scott Moncrieff's translations of Proust would nourish Proust's originals. But the world I live in is pretty messed up. I'd be glad just to think that some of my translations might help to keep their originals from being altogether lost or trashed.

A lot of the translation work I've done has been just exploratory drilling—a little test hole here and there, to try to teach myself a little more about a language I was studying or a text I was learning to read. Many of those translations have never been published and probably shouldn't be. They don't add up to anything more than a series of notes on my own reading. They're things I've done for my own benefit, trying to learn how something worked and trying to see how close I could come in English to something that took my breath away when I saw it done by someone else in another language.

I've worked a little harder at Greek, trying to do some things that might be useful to other people. And I've now spent more than half my life studying Native American languages, translating a few neglected masterpieces and doing some of the background work to make it easier for other people to read them. This isn't going to save the world, but it's my way of trying.

What do you see your translations as doing in the contemporary literary landscape?

You can translate across space, or you can translate across time. The space is sociolinguistic, so the distances involved—physical, cultural, or linguistic—can be large or they can be small. If you translate across time, the time is usually real historical time, and it is usually combined with a lot of linguistic and cultural space. It's translation across time that interests me most, because time, not space, is where I'd otherwise feel cramped.

I see *the present* as a two-dimensional surface. If you live long enough, you get a slight sense of depth, like bas-relief, but still the face of time is essentially flat. You could think of it as a floor that holds you up, or a wall that holds you in, or a window. I'm particularly interested in the window possibility. That's the one form of time travel we have: if you look through the windows of art, science, and literature, you can see your way into the past—and that's your only chance of getting some perspective on the present and the future. That, to me, is the sweetest promise of translation.

In North America, the colonial languages—English, Spanish, French—don't go back very far: only as far as the great campaign to inflict drastic changes on the continent, turning the forests and deserts and grasslands into farms, factories, shopping malls, and amusement parks. Suppose you want to know how people understood this place before that transformation got underway. Suppose you want to know how people saw this place when they loved it, and knew how to live in it, basically just the way it was. To see it through their eyes, you'd need to learn a hundred or more indigenous languages. That's too many; you can't do it. So you'd need some good translations to help you along. A few of the ones you'd need already exist. I'm doing my part to make a few more.

One or two people have told me that this translation campaign is the old colonial enterprise conducted by new means. It's not. Translation doesn't destroy the original—and a good translation doesn't demean or degrade the original; it honours it instead. And if you'll pardon me for harping on the obvious, a good translation of a Native American text honours a Native American viewpoint and a Native American voice. It honours the individual mythteller who dictated the text, and it honours that mythteller's language and culture. Nothing colonial in that.

In your "Leda and the Swan," which I read as a response to Yeats, Leda is more an instrument (xylophone, lute, harp) than young woman. In both poems, she is dehumanized.

Can you tell me about your reading of Leda as a mythological figure?

Leda's story fascinated European painters for several hundred years, but the Greek and Roman poets, who were much closer to it, scarcely touch it. Ovid gives it a single line, Euripides four lines. Homer, Aeschylus, Sophocles, and Euripides spend thousands of lines on the stories of Leda's children and grandchildren, but Leda they leave in the shadows. Could that be just the accidental consequence of what got lost and saved? I don't think so. Maybe the bestiality offended them, though all sorts of human cruelty didn't.

And why did the painters and their patrons, twenty centuries later, swarm around the story? That's maybe an easier question. Voyeurism might be a big factor. Anyway, the painters mostly tell it as a story of seduction. To me, it's a story of rape—and a story about living in a culture where the divinity-in-chief expects to get away with rape. It's also, as I understand it, the story of Leda being raped a second time, on the same day, by her husband, the king. So to me, the crass denial of Leda's humanity is central to the story. If I wrote about Leda and left that out, I'd be lying. But the blindness and cruelty involved aren't the interesting part, so I don't prefer to dwell on them.

For people who think there are no gods, and who feel that humans are the highest form of life, a story with gods in it can be difficult to follow. People in that condition tend to mistake the gods for another tribe of humans. Where people sense that gods exist, gods and humans can interact. But if humans conclude that a god has committed a crime and look for a way to take revenge, it's always other humans, not gods, who end up paying. That's part of Leda's story too.

Leda's a human and Zeus is a god, so there isn't a hope in hell of her resisting his advances. Still, Leda has some powers that Zeus lacks. Her womanhood, her mortality, her humanity, might be powers in this instance, and Zeus's manhood, his one-sidedness, even his immortality might be weaknesses of a kind. Is it possible that Leda teaches Zeus something even as he rapes her? I'm not suggesting that would constitute justice, nor that it's any kind of model for how to deal with human rapists; I'm asking if it could happen.

Leda, as part of keeping herself alive, dreams immediately of revenge—but she can't take revenge on Zeus himself. He's a god and she's a human. She imagines revenge the way she can: through other humans, knowing that the gods might be drawn into that. More blindness and cruelty, if you like—but who could deny her such a wish? The question for me is still whether Zeus could have learned something—not because I sympathize with rapists but because Zeus is a god. I want to know if a human could teach him something.

You've approached the same theme in other poems, such as the first of Arcturus's monologues in *Ursa Minor*. And it appears in "Demons and Men," when you cite Herakleitos: "human culture has no purchase on what is, / but god-culture does." Part of that poem is about the

intermeshing of the classical and the contemporary. Can you say a bit about "god-culture" in our time?

It's a quandary, alright. And if you're looking to start a dialogue between colonial and indigenous traditions in the Americas, it's two quandaries or more.

The missionaries who came to North America in the early days all had some education. They had Latin, often some Greek, and some sense, no matter how condescending, of Roman and Greek paganism. Very few of them shared any of that with their indigenous parishioners. And this got worse, not better, over time. Homer and Virgil weren't taught in the residential schools, and there are no translations of those or any other classical authors into Native American languages. Until the late nineteenth century, there were no translations going the other way either: no Native American narrative poetry coming into a European language. Where there might have been three or four centuries of dialogue between Europeans and Native North Americans—touching, for instance, on nymphs and dryads, river gods and mountain gods, the sacred nature of the earth and the numinous character of landforms—there was confrontation instead. That sea of silence is still with us.

Twenty years ago, when I was writing *Sharp as a Knife*, I felt that I had to try to tackle this question. I also had to find a working vocabulary. A number of my First Nations friends wanted me not to use the word "gods" in translating Native American texts or in talking about them. In the Dinétah—the Navajo country—the word "god" is used routinely but only in certain contexts. *Haashch'ééłti'í*, in

English, is Talking God, *Haashch'ééłchí'í* is Red God, and so on. In many other places—and even for some Navajo—the word is entirely taboo in relation to native tradition. The word "spirit," or "spirit-being," might be acceptable, but the missionaries wanted the word "god" to have one meaning only, and they mostly got their way.

That, in a way, is an easy problem. The meanings exist; the concepts are strong; it's just a question of what words you can use, what noises you can make, that will carry those meanings. In other words, how can you translate the Haida word *sghaana* or the Cree words âtayôhkan and *pawâmiwin* and *manitow*? Translating the Greek *theoi* into Haida, Cree, or Navajo is no problem, if you get the chance to do so.

The problem gets a little harder if you're up against a zealously secular culture—a culture where all the words are free to use but their meanings are lost or forgotten. How do you talk about gods in a society where land is freely bought and sold, where people choose to see the forest as nothing but timber ready for harvest, rivers as nothing but water waiting for someone to build a dam, and where, as Ortega says, Dionysos has been replaced by alcoholism?

There are only a couple of pages in *Sharp as a Knife* that address this question head on, but in a sense, the whole book is my attempt at an answer. And the answer in brief is: Listen to what the people who've lived here longer and know it better have to say about this place. Which people would those be? Not people who meet some genetic criterion but people who've been nourished by a deeply rooted tradition and learned to nourish it in their turn. Skaay, for example. Kâkîsikâw-pîhtokêw, for example. Cháálatsoh, for example. Or Sophocles, for example. Those people never say much about gods. They never give sermons. But everything they say implies their understanding that the world they inhabit is alive and could do with a little respect and affection.

I Know I'm from Here

ANNE COMPTON

Anne Compton was born in Bangor, Prince Edward Island. A two-time winner of the Atlantic Poetry Prize, she won the Governor General's Award for Poetry for *Processional*, her second collection, and the Raymond Souster Award for *Alongside*, her fourth. In 2008, she was awarded the Alden Nowlan Award for Excellence in English Language Literary Arts; and the Lieutenant Governor's Award for High Achievement in English Language Literary Arts in 2014. A former teacher and writer-in-residence at the University of New Brunswick at Saint John, her most recent prose book, *Afterwork: Essays on Literature and Beauty*, appeared in 2017. Her fifth collection, *Smallholding*, was published in 2019. This interview was begun in January 2018. Compton lives in Rothesay, New Brunswick.

There are many poets who travel out and write back to their homes. It seems to me that you've always written out from the home (whether that's PEI or Rothesay). Can you say something about this?

As I have written elsewhere, I assume that every poet, to a greater or lesser degree, writes out of a sense of place, and that "out of" refers not only to the cache of images that "landscapes" his or her mind but also to the need to go beyond, out of, the originating place—a writing away from. The sense of place, moreover, is never synonymous with an actual first place, which, in my case, was Prince Edward Island. For me, the Island is both actual and a source of metaphor. Surrounded by water, and thus an endless horizon, an island necessarily gives an islander a lot to think about in terms of space and time—all that endlessness.

I live, and have lived for almost forty years, however, in rural Rothesay, in a house that overlooks a river with a further shore in sight—wooded, unpopulated—a landscape that, because of changeable, dramatic Bay of Fundy weather, seems a bit different day to day. Almost everything I've published has been written within sight of that river landscape, and every day begins with noting the shifts that have occurred overnight in the look of it due to—depending on the season—the drape of fog or its ice and snow transformations. So, yes, I am embedded in place. Places are starting points for the mind's roaming.

Many of your poems begin from the house and move outward. It seems to me the opposite of a welcoming gesture, yet it is.

I like that word, "outward." I thought there, for a moment, that I was being boxed into the identity of Maritime poet obsessed with past and family. Many of my poems do begin from the house, which is not the same thing as home, with its reverberations of the past. But the thing that bothers me is this: when women poets write about the house, or household doings, reviewers label them "domestic." This doesn't seem to happen with male poets: writing a sonnet about peeling potatoes with his mother, Seamus Heaney is not thereafter referred to as a "domestic" poet. In recent poems, I've been interested in showing all that the house opens onto.

"Unfinished," a newer poem, is very much about the containment of history in the house—and yet again it moves outward.

First of all, I should say that the house in that prose poem is actual; it's a house built around what had once been the workshop of an aeronautical engineer, the inventor of the variable-pitch propeller. Whereas the workshop-turned-room is unlocked, the rest of the house remains unfinished, secured with locks. The room retains its industrial look and its tin ceiling, stencilled in stars, but oddly it's been fitted out with a half dozen gauzy, cloud-looking curtains that sway in the wind entering by way of a pair of propped-open, heavy-duty doors. The speaker wanders in that room, wonders about it, is perplexed by the furnishings, especially the drafting stool pulled up close to a meridian lounge chair, what we would call a day bed—you know, the kind of couch that you might see in a psychoanalyst's office. These two furnishings, so close together, suggest an intimacy, tender or otherwise. Or perhaps they are arranged that way as a kind of memorial. The room is vacant. There's never anyone there. The history of its complex decor is unknown to her, yet familiarly haunts her. The poem is exploring the link between house interiors and the mind's interior—the unconscious. A single room can be, for a writer, the beginning of an outward movement, the contemplation of things that go way beyond the domestic, but a room can also lead inward—to "what we know but shouldn't know," as the poem says. In the last paragraph of the poem, the speaker is shown into (so to speak) the unfinished, locked-up house.

Virginia Woolf wrote in her "Letter to a Young Poet" that poetry "has never been used for the common purpose of life. Prose has taken all the dirty work onto her own shoulders." Do your domestic poems (and Heaney's) suggest otherwise?

I don't know if Woolf indicates the "domestic" in her phrase "dirty work," but I do know that when money was scarce and she had to choose between hiring a servant (a cook/cleaner) and the cost of plumbing, she chose the servant. More interesting is her separation of poetry and "the common purpose of life": one of poetry's jobs is, surely, to recognize the uncommon, even the extraordinary, within the common. The "domestic" is usually equated with the homely and the commonplace, consisting of those tasks done by drudges and dullards when, in fact, "domestic" routines can be approached as rituals. In Heaney's sonnet, the speaker's recalled boy-self chose the ritual of kitchen work with his mother instead of the ritual of the Mass with the rest of the family. Heaney's poem aligns, while discriminating, different kinds of rituals.

There's nothing wrong, and everything right, about household routines. It's the delimiting use of the word "domestic" that I object to, as if "real" poetry can only be composed by people free of those jobs and tasks as Wordsworth was in hallowing the "real language of men." In his poem "To My Sister," inviting her to join him outdoors for the "blessed power" of nature, he says, "Now that our morning meal is done, / Make haste your morning task resign." We know who was doing the washing up there! But, wait, Dorothy Wordsworth was a poet. Her sentences made their way into his poetry. And Emily Dickinson wrote poems on scraps of paper that she stuffed into her apron while she cooked and cleaned. The "domestic" isn't an impediment to poetry; it's one of its environments, and as Heaney so rightly recognizes, it may very well be the better ritual.

Connected to the question above is, in my mind, the way in which poetry and family intertwine in your work. I think of the father in "What Light Decays," who could be your own father or a Virgil-like guide. Are there risks in poeticizing one's family?

There are no more risks in writing about family than there are in writing about lovers or mates, friends or acquaintances, characters you've come across in literature, or the figures in paintings. Prisoners of a single consciousness, we are endlessly interested in others' minds, and we can only know about those minds from people's behaviours, their responses to us, or by what they report of their thoughts and feelings. That interest in others' minds always begins where life begins—with siblings and parents. I believe that you call that interest in another's mind, to the extent that we can ever know it, being human. In my case, growing up in a household of ten siblings, I witnessed a vast array of behaviours, benefitted from the reported thoughts and feelings of some dozen people.

Can you say more about what you mean by "mind"?

You're asking me to define "mind!" Put five neuroscientists in a room and you'll get five different definitions of "mind." One will talk about the millions of neurons in the brain, its billions of synapses; another will talk about the inter-relationship of the lobes; and eventually all five will have a punch-out over the question "Does brain make mind?"

In my response to your previous question, I meant mind in the everyday sense: you have a mind, I have one. But in spite of the fact that you are talking to me—revealing certain things about your mind through your questions—I don't know, can't ever really know, the thoughts and feelings occurring in your mind. I'm a bit obsessed, as you can see, by this idea that the mind makes solitaries of us all. Many creatures have mind, but humans have minds endowed with consciousness, and it's consciousness that unites and separates us humans. Unites us because we have that possession in common (at least when we are awake) and because it enables us to be aware of, and report on, our thoughts and feelings, but it is a very limited report that we can give.

Lyric poets, you might think, put their consciousness on the page, but always when the poem's done, there's the feeling you've failed to convey your thoughts and feelings. Most poets would attribute that to the slippage between mind and word, but it's more likely due to the fact that although we're consciously aware of what's passing in our minds, we can't access the spontaneous unconscious emotions that exist beneath thoughts and feelings, and, second, after we've written the poem and go back to it in revision, we can't get back to what passed in the mind— consciousness being so fluid—when we created the poem in the first place.

I suppose I was wondering about the way in which family is mythical in your poems rather than simply biographical. That is, Eliotic rather than Confessional.

I'm surprised when juries and critics put poetry in the non-fiction category. Poetry fictionalizes as much as novels and short stories do, although poems begin—at least for me—in an autobiographically noticed or recalled sight or sound. An acute perceptual moment can send you off on a poem and send you anywhere. As for your comment about the mythical and family in my poems, yes, that's so, but then the mythic nature of my family was something of a given because of its history, structure, and religious background. I've said little, and will be saying little, about my family backstory (the generations before my own). I've confined my attention to siblings and parents, but even there, I've been a storyteller, aware of the mythic light cast upon them by those things.

Can we take this "mythic light" back to your poem "What Light Decays"? That is, can you say a bit about the father in that poem?

In this ghost poem, the speaker, near to sleep, hears her dead father call, believes herself, of all the living, the chosen one. She makes her way to him, this boatman of the river, her fisherman father, who will tell her, she hopes, where he has come from. But, it seems, it's this life he wants, gruffly asking about her mother's whereabouts. Father and daughter are in an in-between place where time and foothold are unsteady. So, yes, it's a mythic landscape, and the father, in his supposed other-world knowledge, is part Charon and, maybe, part Agamemnon. Re-reading the poem just now, the Agamemnon similarity struck me. The daughter has become a "What" to the father: "*What are you?*" And she fears she will be un-daughtered: will lose "the daughter to gain a guide." But the Christian story is here too, a Calvinist one. She believes she is "chosen." This, you understand, is all afterthought, this sourcing. A visual memory of my father, smoking a cigarette by his rowboat, took me into the poem. My father, who loved fishing, taught me how to remove the hook from the fish's mouth, how to gut and cook it, and how to row a boat. Shouldn't a father, even in death, have something further to tell?

Can we talk about form? I think of sonnets, glosas, the ghazals of *Processional* (2005). How does form begin as regards the writing of a poem?

For me, the first line or two of the poem—originating in something heard or seen or in an image recalled—will determine form. I take my cue from those first lines. Of the kinds you mention, the glosa is the one sort of poem that is form-led. Sometimes another poet's lines will nag me in such a way that I am forced to think it through in verse. The glosa allows me to do that expansively, but in a controlled way. I have, however, a broad sense of form. Beyond the received forms, I believe that a poem that works out a metaphor, or a pattern of metaphors, in a taut, controlled way through the length of the poem, is formal. Similarly, an idea introduced, returned to, threaded through the whole gives a poem a formal dimension. Above all—to speak of pattern now rather than form—a pattern of interlocking sounds is what gives a poem not only its coherence but also its force. When I'm reading poetry, it is the poet's orchestration of sound that I find most affective. And when that sound pattern coincides with, and reinforces, the build of images or an evolving metaphor, you have a poem that enters your memory without your ever actively memorizing it. Pattern bestows memorability on a poem.

Following on from that, tell me about long lines. Why do you think this element has become so important in your work? Is it their capability to convey narrative?

I like a loping syntax, but I also seem to create rather a lot of sentence fragments, and I love the relationship between the two, the way the former expands upon the fragmentary. It seems to me that mix is the way we speak to one another—short, quick responses followed by an elaboration so that the longer surprises us even as we are working it out, takes us unaware. My long-lined poems are an effect of those thinking-through sentences that emerge, or grow, from the fragments. But those long lines also indicate, as you suggest, my story-telling inclination. The individual lyric poem has a narrative spine, and often in reading someone's poetry, you can find a narrative line—either a story line or a narrative of ideas—across the whole book. My long lines, though, are also connected to my tilt toward the auditory. Even though I am an endless note taker of what is visibly around me, the auditory is most often my starting point. I ventriloquize people's speech habits—their idioms and sayings, and of course that inclination to set down their speech patterns is connected to narrative, the larger story that lurks within how they speak, the way, for example, East Coast Canadians and Americans use the word "some" as a modifier, "some cold," and other times use that word for "somewhat," delaying its position in the sentence, as in "the day's dark was like midnight, some."

Even though my poetry has that narrative ambition, I think it's also important to say—I'm thinking now about the brain—that language in poetry functions differently from linear-driven fiction and from the logical, sequential argument of an essay. Language happens in the left brain hemisphere, but because of its musicality and because of its drive toward form and its visual image density, poetry requires the use of both hemispheres. Music and visual imagery and our spatial sense are located in the right hemisphere. Poetry, either making it or reading it, requires that we access and move between the two hemispheres. The poet's use of metaphor, which, as far as I'm concerned, is the very essence of poetry, is something I don't understand with regard to the brain. How that lightning-strike bringing together of the "strange unlike" happens is a mystery to me.

Can you tell me a bit about the difference, then, not just in the writing but also the reading, between prose and poetry as you see it?

I don't know about you, but I have to read poetry first thing in the morning. I need my most wide-awake, flexible mind for poetry. I read fiction last thing at night. A novel—I'm speaking here in the most general terms—

gives you, after you get your bearings in it, a populated world you can keep returning to and the momentum of a plot to keep you there. The novel, like the theatre—but without the apparatus of a film or stage theatre—darkens down your immediate surrounding and absorbs you into its world. And I don't mean it's escapist. One of the virtues of the novel is its creation of whole worlds—alternative, though recognizable, worlds, complete with cupboards and city streets or whatever. By contrast, the lyric poem is scrappy (both senses of the word). It's partial—rigorously focused as opposed to broadly depictive. It makes you work harder and is, therefore, less welcoming than the novel. The poem's condensed, compact, yet home to multiple meanings, meanings that the reader has to keep in mind over the length of the poem, meanings that accrue not just by virtue of the metaphors and other tropes but also because of sound patterns that execute connections line to line and line breaks that can alter the reading of a preceding or following line. Nonetheless, a poem's smallest unit of thought—a three-word phrase, a single line, the flare of an image—can short-circuit the tangled wiring of possible meanings and illumine the whole. If you think about what's entered our talk and gets quoted in lectures, speeches, and everyday conversation, it's most often lines of poetry, not prose. A poem can be mind-altering and not just because of what it says but because of how it says it: reading poetry trains us in mental agility. There are, of course, novels that have a similar effect. Virginia Woolf's, for example. Still, what I want from both forms, novel and poem, is to be emotionally affected.

What's the value of that: to be "emotionally affected"? Is it something people need in their lives, do you think? Or is it a more elite sensation?

Oh, it's a need and not at all elite. The sight of the father cardinal feeding his fledglings on the verandah rail is "emotionally affecting," as is a great poem. We all need—wherever we can get it—what is complicatedly tender and touched by mortality and yet a source of hope. I do quite a bit of reading about the visual arts, and I notice that one line of art criticism these days—perhaps the dominant one—approaches the artwork as a thought puzzle; as Arthur C. Danto says, "What you've got to try to do is see the work, any work, as a piece of thought. As an art critic, very much like a philosopher, you're concerned with the logical clarification of that thought…" I don't know if there is a parallel, and similar, priority given to "thought" in poetry criticism, but if there is, I'd disagree with it. There's no hierarchy: thought is not superior to feeling, and neither is it lower; it is not prior to feeling and it does not lag. In a poem, the intelligence communicates—manages, arranges, illumines—the emotional content through the word choices, the run of syntax, pattern and form, quickness and pause. A poem is not intelligent because it brings in, say, references to science or philosophical ideas; it's intelligent in the way it works out what it has to say. Thought and feeling aren't really separable, but I think that the emotional affect arrives first when you're reading a poem. That has to do with cadence.

So many of your poems are driven by desire. Is that an important starting place for your writing? I think of the opening section of *Alongside* (2013), with its longing for mind and body of another poet.

Yes, that section of *Alongside* lays bare what energized all the previous poems—an unrealizable desire. But are there, you have to wonder, any other kinds? If hope is "the evidence of things unseen," how much more is desire the "evidence" of things unachievable. Those poems are about a desire for a beloved, a desire that can never bring the pair into proximity and that can never end. Didn't Rilke say that the most we can do is guard one another's solitude? Maybe that kind of long-lasting intellectual-erotic desire is a type for all other desires—the desire for the beautiful, the desire for something—an emotional aliveness—that supersedes our ordinary wants and yet lifts those wants, and the actions that flow from them, beyond the commonplace so that setting the table for supper or putting the spring seeds in the ground seems the most important thing that you could be doing. As one of those poems says, he was "A voice summoning me to the surface, to attention…"

Where does that critical voice fit into all of this? You are that rare hybrid, poet-critic, and this is part of both your prose and poetry. Do the poet and critic get along? Or are they binaries?

Poet and critic get along nicely, although the poet would be my first self and the critic my second. They are mutually supportive, even if the poet nourishes the critic more than the critic does the poet. The poet teaches the critic how to read—slowly, savouringly—and also teaches the critic to keep her voice tuned to everyday speech and avoid the high-falutin'. There are differences and similarities between them. The critic, when she's about, is selfish, taking all the attention and the mental energy. Second, the poet will just up and go away, leave for rather long periods, whereas the critic is always available. You can call on her at any time. Third, the critic has to assume a certain authority, look like she knows what she's talking about; the poet can proceed in uncertainty. The truth, though, is that the critic, for all her pose as know-it-all, is also writing to find out. Nonetheless, they've established something like a sibling satisfaction in one another's company. The critic, not by what she writes but by what she reads in order to write, enlarges the poet's way of thinking about things and introduces strange new metaphors.

Finally, I think we need to talk about "talk," so central to your interviews, your essays, and your poems. In a new poem, "Talk Puts an End to Time," you write about a speaker in an empty hall, a number of buildings left behind, as the speaker steps out. And you conclude, "On a day of steady rain, how to summon it back, be of it?"

It's ironic, isn't it, I claim to be a recluse, or semi-recluse, yet I've spent so much of my life in "talk." That poem looks at my earlier self: podium-me, lecturer and conference presenter. It's about the vanity of the lecturer, the person who lives in the first-person, the "I" who excludes the "we"; the "I" who wants to impress with her talk, talk, talk. In the first part of the poem, the lecturer realizes she's talking to an empty room (the audience gone) and realizes as well that while she's been holding forth, time has hidden the housefronts in overgrown hedges, emptied the warehouses on the waterfront. The world's vacated, and she's responsible for that. But then she remembers (part three of the poem) an occasion, years back, when an emptied building, a deserted barn, mysteriously retained the rustle of the animals that had once been there. Because of that memory, she knows that time keeps "Presence," that, in spite of the fact her vanity has emptied the hall, emptied the world of "Presence," she could get back to a peopled world—windows lit with their lives and busyness—if only she could figure out "how to summon it back." The poem expresses my suspicion that public performances, and that includes poetry readings, are more about the ego of the performer and less about reaching out to an audience, a community. Public performance is, therefore, an oxymoron. Occasionally, you have the feeling you've led the wrong life. Maybe the poem is also suggesting that.

Sometimes, in the middle of a poetry reading, I have the feeling that I'm betraying the poems, turning them into performance, my physical voice overtopping, falsifying the poems. But that may be a different issue.

The Civilizing Discourse

NYLA MATUK

Nyla Matuk was born in Winnipeg and raised in Ottawa. She holds an MA in English from McGill University with a thesis on the philosopher Charles Taylor's theory of art and moral sources. She is the author of two books of poetry: *Sumptuary Laws* (2012) and *Stranger* (2016). She is also the editor of an anthology of poems, *Resisting Canada* (2019). In 2014, she attended Yaddo artists' residency in the United States and in 2018, she served as the Mordecai Richler Writer in Residence at McGill University. Her identity obtains from lands to which her ancestors belong, located in India, Bokhara, Afghanistan, and Palestine. She works for the Department of Canadian Heritage arts sector and lives in Tiohtià:ke, known also as Montreal. This interview was conducted via email between 18 June and 9 July 2022.

Your poems have always been critical in their thinking—but beginning with the 2019 anthology you edited, *Resisting Canada*, there is a clearer political agenda. What were your motivations for putting the anthology together?

The motivation for the anthology is rooted in my curiosity about the variability of poetry—how language might be both compelling and accountable outside matters tending to the personal, and how it might address the urgency of collective political consciousness with the consideration of social conditions. Or perhaps a consciousness of injustice. My political or justice awakening—a noticeable uptick in such consciousness—began in 2014, when, for fifty-one days, the world watched the merciless bombing of Palestinian refugees living in the region of historic Palestine known as Gaza, under blockade since 2006.

Watching those fifty-one days via Twitter and other media left me physically numb and psychologically horrified. At the same time, more of the brutal history of residential schools in so-called Canada was being uncovered through the published memoirs of elders, Indigenous journalism, and academic studies. The reckoning of settler colonialism in at least two of its iterations—Canada and Israel—was all around us then and has continued to make itself known.

My own poetry stood in stark contrast to the resistance poems I started to read to curate *Resisting Canada*. What emerged for me, and what I continue to think about as I have turned to writing fiction, is the irreconcilable tension between private experience and collective consciousness. Matters of collective knowledge I focused on were Palestine's ongoing anti-colonial national liberation movement and the history of Indigenous peoples closer to where I grew up. Coming of age in a settler colony in the '70s and '80s, I perceived literary culture as fixated on works that take the individual romantic subject as the point of view and often as subject matter. The anthology offered an alternative.

Most of the contemporary poetry I had been reading worked in that individuated register, not particularly aware of systemic oppression. Perhaps the latter makes too much purpose out of poetry and is therefore deservedly overlooked, or maybe we have not moved out of a need to find common cause with personal matters, another individual's hardships, joy, existential crisis, or the desire to discover a kindred spirit or friend at the end of a collection of poems?

I wanted to know how language—and poems in particular—could express something other than the travails and temperaments of the Kierkegaardian Individual, the lone figure of the bildungsroman, and so forth. I'm not sure that any of the poems I included fit the bill, but this discrepancy was top of mind.

Can you say more about the notion of "common cause"?

I meant that readers may seek a dyadic relationship with the poet, to find common cause in personal anguish, grief, or wonder and laughter (maybe that sounds a bit too much like "Live! Love! Laugh!"). "Common cause" may be the wrong description here—empathic consciousness is perhaps what I want to say.

As for poetry that sketches collective consciousness—systems of oppression felt in the face of, for example, colonial destruction—it may be seen as didactic, or perhaps it's just a different valence of private experience: one's private experience of the violence done to one's own people. Depending on the way the work is written, it could be seen as didactic (teaching moment), but I do see that didacticism present in poetry that expresses private experience too—*here is my tragedy, I am alone with this, and there is no mentionable reason, but please empathize; here is my tow-headed child sitting in a patch of sunlight with our new kitten. I want to teach you how vulnerable they are.*

The private can be political, though?

Yes, in a way I have created a false dilemma. I have been reading Mahmoud Darwish's *Memory for Forgetfulness*. As Beirut is terrorized, as the bombs drop, we are invited into the poet's daily ritual of coffee preparation, for instance. The personal minutia here meets the larger canvas of terror, despair, imperialist assault.

There are lots of examples from Mahmoud Darwish of the private experience of living under occupation and settler colonialism. In reader-response criticism, we may not wish to use those sociological/political terms and focus instead on the poet's craft, aspects of the way the personal is sketched. Another example of this kind of expression is found in the poems of Maya Abu al-Hayyat, *You Can Be the Last Leaf* (translated by Fady Joudah). In her review of that collection, Lena Khalaf Tuffaha writes,

Despite her belief in art "as reparation for love and wisdom," Abu Al-Hayyat's poems remain firmly planted in the realities of a colonized homeland. In "Massacres," the state of siege that marks all Palestinian life is laid bare:

> Massacres teach me not to wait for
> those who'll be pulled out of the rubble
> and not to follow the stories of survivors.
> I go on with my day without pausing for wonders.

This sensibility marks a myriad of fictional works by the great Palestinian writer, journalist, and revolutionary Ghassan Kanafani.

How has this affected your own work and thinking?

On my quest to find an alternative to the Strong Voice of an Individual, ironically, I turned to the idea of identity. One's identity as a person with Indigenous roots opens a political or a justice consciousness, questions that perforce move us beyond individuation. There is a collective consciousness. That led me to an interest in the history of one side of my family, the Palestinian side. As soon as I started to learn more about the people in my family, it was impossible to separate them from the wider history of the Palestinian people in the nineteenth and twentieth centuries. I couldn't write about my family members without realizing that the fragmented nature of their recollections, and the elliptical nature of what could be known about them—the knowledge of them that

I could shore up—was inextricably bound to the wider history of colonial violence and anti-colonial resistance to European imperialist designs on the Levant region, the bilad a-sham.

It was startling, then, to read Edward Said's description of Palestinian literature: "Our characteristic mode ... is not a narrative in which scenes take place *seriatim*, but rather broken narratives, fragmentary compositions, and self-consciously staged testimonials in which the narrative voice keeps stumbling over itself, its obligations and its limitations."

As I read books on the history of Al Quds (Jerusalem) and travelled in Palestine, I came across many mentions: people, places from the photos in those books, and from the stories my father told me. The street wall, in the photo of my father outside his home before the Nakba, was right there, miraculously, outside the window of my hotel. The photo is dated 1945. How strange to see the bullet holes in the aluminum wall in front of the girls' grammar school, that my father mentioned, as I walked beside it in his former neighbourhood. How strange to discover an archive of unpublished *National Geographic* photos on Instagram and find many members of my own family in 1974 in the house not yet demolished in the Old City. Apparently, it stood alongside three other houses, as late as 1974, following Israel's ethnic cleansing and destruction of the rest of the neighbourhood—the twelfth-century Mughrabi (Moroccan) Quarter—in 1967.

Pieces of oneself, one's family, in history, in documentation, and in real life. This has affected my poetic consciousness, though it is surely not uniquely Palestinian.

I don't know. Mostly it is this return to history—and literal return to the land in the case of Palestine—that directs my poems because this larger reality is impossible to ignore given the forced displacement of the Palestinian people. There is a through line running from every Palestinian's life to the Nakba. The "lost ground of our origins" is forever discoverable in writing and perceiving.

The phrase enables us to begin to scratch the surface of the potentialities of Indigenous poetries; writing from the condition of exile or the loss of ground—the land— where Indigenous people belong recuperates the seeds of revolution that would upend settler-colonial culture and the belief in the nobility and purity of the settler-colony state and the culture of those who came in the wake of those imperialist invasions. No wonder Canadian state media, the CBC, told my publisher that *Resisting Canada* "is not for us" and would not give it any attention.

To be honest, I am not sure to what extent I have at all been affected stylistically in my own work except to say that I prefer to write about this stuff through fiction and nonfiction rather than poetry. I am not sure why. Poetry of the kind I wrote in *Sumptuary Laws* is bedecked with grandiloquence, lyricism, bombast, mannered poses, decorative excess, rhyme and alliteration, nursery rhymes and nonsense verse, and my imitative/parodic assay on high aesthetics and stylized writings. My inspirations were Wallace Stevens, Elizabeth Bishop, and T.S. Eliot, for instance, Ashbery, Mlinko and others.

Whatever poetry I have written about Palestine has been rooted in my extensive reading of its history—

particularly the last 150 years. This period of colonialism on Palestine is arguably the most brutal, according to the historian and researcher Salman Abu-Sitta. At this time, on social media and elsewhere on any given day, one witnesses video footage of Palestinians defending their land against settlers and the Israeli forces that work to protect illegal activity the settlers carry out as deputized agents of the state. The settler activity is no different than that of the settlers who were deputized to steal land from Indigenous peoples in North America, Turtle Island. The Nakba begun against the Palestinian people in 1947/48 has not stopped.

I don't think I've found a way to express all this in poetry to my satisfaction, as if writing poetry, for me, begun as something quite other, cannot now be transposed to "history from below." Of course, many poets have expressed dispossession quite beautifully. I'm thinking, for instance, of Lena Khalaf Tuffaha's "Mountain, Stone" from her collection *Water & Salt*:

> Do not name your daughters Shaymaa,
> courage will march them
> into the bullet path of dictators.
>
> Do not name them Sundus,
> the garden of paradise calls out to its marigolds,
> gathers its green leaves up in its embrace.
>
> Do not name your children Malak or Raneem,
> angels want the companionship of others like them,
> their silvery wings trailing the filth of jail cells,
> the trill of their laughter a call to prayer....

…Do not name your children. Let them live
nameless, seal their eyelids
and sell their voices to the nightingale.

Do not name your children
and if you must
call them by what withstands

this endless season of decay.
Name them mountains,
call them stone.

I'm also thinking of Mahmoud Darwish's *In the Presence of Absence* and *Mural*. The Gaza scholar and writer Haider Eid has described his own process in literature seminars as a mode of inquiry springing from the standpoint of the colonized and how it provides an alternative to the official—that is, more dominant—version of history of the colonizer. "We then compare Palestinian and South African history and conclude that Apartheid and Zionism both created a dominant historical narrative that sought to eliminate all other narratives." In this way, poetry is also political consciousness, knowledge.

The definition of Said's that you began with is Eliotic— that's "The Waste Land." How might your own poem, "On Palaces," fit into this discussion?

"On Palaces" was written in part about Orient House, located in East Jerusalem on Abu Obeida Street, a house that belongs to the Husayni family, a political-class, elite Jerusalem dynasty—perhaps to be considered Palestinian nobility. The Orient House served later as the headquarters of the Palestine Liberation Organization, until 2001, when it was seized by the Israelis and looted of historic documents. I read about it in a book on Jerusalem and came to see the site on my visit in 2020; in the same book, I found evidence of family members: for example, a great-uncle who was for decades a football and athletic coach at the nearby St. George's School and the Friends School in Ramallah. The whole family—the men, anyway—attended St. George's. There are other landmarks in the area too, a couple of palaces bearing my great-grandmother's surname and presumably the seat of her family, and so on.

So I think my stumbling, to borrow Said's idea, my fragmentary narrative, to think on Eliot, is larger history as a backdrop for the fragments I have shored against my, or my familial, ruins. I have picked up other fragments reading other texts as well, such as the role my elders played in the Battle of Sheikh Jarrah of 1948, an important site of resistance that could be considered the theatre of Palestinian victory against Zionist incursions on Al Quds. I know about these people because they are directly connected to relatives in Canada—this too is the fragment, embodied. The looting and other history recounted in "On Palaces" traces the importance of materiality to the colonial condition—this history is directly connected to people, to papers, archives, stone and mortar. It's through a materialist historical framework that we can best understand the machinations of imperial violence and trace that violence on the land—including urban places—to the attempted erasure of a people. Many of the funeral processions of prominent Palestinians martyred in 1948 began at the Orient House. In 1949, it served as the headquarters of the United Nations Relief and Works Agency (UNRWA), a United Nations office specifically created in the wake of the transformation of so many Palestinians living in their own homeland to "Palestine refugees." Again, this history cements the condition of being Palestinian in concrete ways.

What is the connection for you between poetry and history?

Knowing one's history lends authenticity to one's narratives—one's personal history but, equally importantly, the history of one's roots: how one's family arrived at the place they were at when one was a child, experiencing everything for the first time. If, as the American poet Louise Glück has written, "we see the world once, in childhood' / the rest is memory," what lurks in that memory? The memory of my mother's high cheekbones and almond-shaped eyes, for instance, might draw me to the characteristic physiognomy of her people, in Central Asia, the mountains north of Kabul and the region of Bokhara. Under what colonial conditions do those people live today? How has the present condition been established?

I do not mean to cancel the idea of a mannered or stylish form of expression when I say we strive for authenticity—

rather that there is a buttress, a scaffolding that history provides for the creative expression of poetry, narrative arts, and other types of language art. It is out of social conditions that art is produced, not out of some disengaged and dematerialized encounter of a divine nature. The poet is not outside of the conditions of history. There are material conditions and cause and effect that may connect poetry with history. I say this in contradistinction to French Symbolism and German Romanticism, not, perhaps, in opposition to Wordsworth.

Is understanding of history, then, a way to create a poem that doesn't sound touristic? "On Palaces" certainly doesn't, yet it has that element to it.

Sometimes, as in the Palestinian case which is once again pertinent to your broader inquiry, one may witness what has happened *only* as a tourist, not only because one may not have access to normally accessible archival material (so much of Palestine's records were destroyed or remain confiscated) but because the trauma of the Nakba means that it can be very difficult to ask those who lived through it—now quite elderly—to produce an oral history. Luckily, the latter exists anyway, in recorded narratives. As far as I'm aware, these are mostly rendered in Arabic. Millions of Palestinians are not permitted to enter Palestine at all, so they can't even go to their ancestral homeland as tourists. Many in Gaza and Lebanon camps live in walking distance or a short drive from the homes they were forced to flee. They are barred and remain in those camps waiting for their inalienable right of return to be granted. Return, "al-awda," is the heart of the Palestine matter.

The aspiration of being a returnee surpasses "witness" and "tourist." I think one can sound like a tourist—enter the territory as a tourist—and still understand history, still become a witness. Being a tourist may sound less authentic, but if you are a tourist with blood ties and historic belonging, then it may be that one's tourism feels like something more profound, that is, being a witness. My own experience of being in Sheikh Jarrah, reading about my relatives' roles in the Battle of Sheikh Jarrah in 1948 and, two years after my visit, watching video footage on Twitter of the same battle continuing, added another dimension to the act of being a witness. The personal is political.

You mentioned above that you prefer fiction and non-fiction for your writings on Palestine, yet "1948," a newer poem, has its declarations and intentions: "Who spoke be-fore the planners of towers, private agencies? / Before mandate, civilizing committee, Declaration, / billionaire American, capital, and colony hotel?" And its own music and mannerisms, especially around polysyllabic language. Your work suggests the two things can mix in poetry.

I find it difficult to write about serious subjects using the conventions of English poetry—rhyming couplets, for instance. This is not to say that some formal devices might not work very well in formal register—the villanelle, for instance, even the pantoum. When I think of the sound making the sense, I think of wonder about, for example, a seashell, the sunlight striking the underside of clouds, the sound of waves, a spring morning of damp grass and robins. Maybe I have chosen trite examples, but I place wonder into a separate category from rumination. Awe, or even Wordsworth's emotion recollected in tranquility, is not the same as rumination, anger, resistance against the nexus of imperial power trying to destroy you or steal your home. And so I arrived at the idea that I prefer fiction or non-fiction prose for such expression. But clearly many poets excel with this, so it's really a reflection on my limits! Matthew Arnold would disagree.

Are there limits to what a poem can do, you think?

One can use language in thousands of ways—perhaps this is limitless. But language is "always already," it is always removed from the immediacy of a happening. It can record, it records after the fact. To inhabit it is to admit to a deadened condition. It's dead, there on the page, recounting what happened off the page. For these reasons, it's a powerful, or maybe I could say homeopathic, conduit for expressing trauma, which we might twin with shame—always hidden and removed from view and from the present. I am thinking of the long poem in D.M. Thomas's *The White Hotel*, where history, both personal and shared, is a major element.

In an essay he based on the introduction to his translation of Jan Zábrana's *The Lesser Histories*, Justin Quinn wrote:

W.B. Yeats was surely wrong when he wrote that "[w]
e make out of the quarrel with others, rhetoric, but of
the quarrel with ourselves, poetry." This suggests that
poetry, in its essence, has no public dimension, that the
realms of politics, of community, of shared experiences
more generally, don't belong in the genre, which is better
suited to expressions of the inner spirit. Of course, the
first place to look for evidence that Yeats was wrong is
in his own poetry. Many of his poems resonated, and
still resonate, in public forums, while others that talk of
love and of spirit make some fine rhetorical moves. Still,
the dictum can't quite be discounted, as it suggests that
poetry can somehow reach deeper into the spirit than
any other literary genre.

I don't buy that dictum, because I've read countless beau-
tiful sentences and their beauty moved me as much as
lineated cadence. They were in fiction, in criticism, in
essays, probably even newspaper articles.

The Poems Stolen from Me Line by Line

IMAN MERSAL

Iman Mersal was born in northern Egypt and emigrated to Canada in 1999, becoming a citizen in 2007. She is the author of five poetry collections in Arabic, a selection from which was translated by Robyn Creswell and published in 2022 as *The Threshold*. She has also published *How to Mend: Motherhood and Its Ghosts* (2019), which weaves a new narrative of motherhood through diaries, readings, and photographs. Mersal's work has also appeared in *The Paris Review, The New York Review of Books*, and *The Nation*. Her nonfiction novel, *Traces of Enayat*, appeared in 2023. She works as an associate professor of Arabic literature and Middle Eastern studies at the University of Alberta. This interview was conducted between February 10 and September 19, 2023. Mersal lives in Edmonton.

I'd like to begin by asking about form: Robyn Creswell mentions in his introduction that all of your poems begin in prose. How do you decide on line breaks? Is it visual, metrical, syntactical?

The break in a prose poem is all of the above. Its body appears on the surface of the page, which it does not fully occupy because it has its own shape, line arrangements, breaks, or simply "private spaces." For me as a reader, each prose poem is distinguished like an individual creature; each has its specific structure, features, and imagination. Prose poems seem to give the poet great freedom, but the poet gives the poem many invisible roles that constrain her. For example, the poet might believe that imagination should be specific. Then that specificity would require much effort from poet and translator alike.

You can imagine a voice whispering the poem to you or reading it aloud. A voice needs to accelerate, to slow, to breathe, and sometimes to pause. A line break in a poem is not a performative tool, but it is part of a poem's identity.

When you try to carry a voice from one language to another, you face so many challenges, including musicality of the original language and its particular writing spaces. Robyn Creswell was always interested in locating each poem's tone of voice; he patiently found solutions within the poem's original structure. By reading a poem such as "The State," you can see the work behind keeping the streamlined one-sentence poem without breathing or pausing in the middle, while in a poem such as "Celebration," the challenge was to keep moving between two different images with their different tones of speech that characterize this poem. One of the exercises I enjoyed during the translation process was reading a poem in Arabic to Robyn and listening to him reading the translation in English and then reflecting on its arrangement and musicality.

This is interesting. Usually writers talk about "voice" as singular, but what you're suggesting here is that each poem has its own voice?

Let us imagine the writer's voice as a thread of light stretching between what is written and what is read, between intention and interpretation. The voice of a writer, or any person, is the continuity of something that shifts, switches its tone; the tone of cynicism in youth isn't the same as that of the parent of youth. Let us also imagine a voice with an accent: the accent vibrating around this thread, not fully congruent with it. Sometimes these vibrations intensify the light, strengthening the original intention; at other times, they disrupt the light or threaten to block it entirely. The existence of each poem requires a distinctive tone of voice, its mood, or accent.

Following on from that, how, for you, are poetry and prose (by which I also mean the poetic and prosaic) intertwined and/or separated?

Maybe it is impossible to separate poetry and prose; they are always intertwined in fine writing. However, we recognize poetry when it exists in any given text, orality, or even dreams, with all of our senses. Poetry is not about ideas; it involves our memory and being when we encounter it.

As someone who writes in different genres, I feel poetry is the most challenging. Poetry is unpredictable; you can't force it, saying, "Hey, I have a day off so I will write a poem." In my experience, editing is an important stage in writing, but it's different with poetry. You can't save a poem by editing it again and again. Poems are fragile; if a poem is not authentic, edits will not save it.

Can you say something about the process of working with your translator, Robyn Creswell?

The translation is Robyn's work; I see my contribution in the dialogue over poems that turned into a friendship. If I have anything to say, it will be about what I learned through the process, not only about the English language but about Arabic and my writing as well. *The Threshold* is a selection from four poetry books, the first of them published in 1995. There were at least two different kinds of sensibilities, two different moments in my life as well as in modern Arabic poetry. Robyn was already quite familiar with my later poetry; he had to work harder to capture the anger, frustrations, playfulness, and sense of humour in the earlier poems. He had to learn about the 1990s Arabic landscape: the complex feelings that imbue the poetry of a specific historical moment socially, politically, and stylistically—to maintain these qualities in his translation without having to elaborate or explain them. How Robyn worked through these different moments was inspiring for me; he somehow translated the context in the background of words.

Our dialogue included discussions about the order of the poems in a selection from multiple books. I'd already gone through the process of arranging these poems in Arabic for each book, but in arranging *The Threshold*, we had to look across a much bigger span of time and poetry. This was a fun part of the process; a chronological order would have been easy but is not the most interesting way. How do they all sound in English? How can we maintain continuity of voice? But at a certain point, we might also want there to be a contrast or a silence between two poems.

Creating new continuities and contrasts was important in this work. We had the ability to decide.

What resulted was a sequence of different moods. Perhaps they are different voices, or perhaps a single voice, progressing over time.

In "A Life," from *The Threshold*, there is a list of losses, one of which is "the poems stolen from me line by line until I doubted whether they were ever mine." Does this connect to the different voices you mentioned?

Well, maybe. It is difficult to justify your choices in a poem, but I will try. "A Life" is a poem about recognizing and conceding time: a woman who awakes in a strange land one day to find herself entering the age of forty. It is an attempt to understand, accept, reconcile with aging. It is also a playful poem; fragments from her past include doubts about her past writing. I don't think I was aware of these choices while writing this poem, but I see as a reader that contemplating the fragments from this past life are not citations from previous poems about the same fragments. Rather, there is a dialogue with other texts (the Quran, where God has never chosen a woman for prophecy; a poem by Mahmoud Darwish, who wrote about a woman entering her forties with "her perfect apricots"; Milosz, who felt a door opening in him and he entered). The dialogue with other texts seems necessary to widen this "I," to give up for a moment what she wrote before as if what is written before belongs now to others.

There is much in your poems about the modern life of a poet: working in a university, being a mother, travelling to literary events. Some of it is alienation, but there is also guilt, as in "An Essay on Children's Games." Can you say something about this? It seems contradictory.

I don't see this as contradictory; motherhood, migration, mobility, one's writing career, even recognition carry within them different kinds of guilt. In motherhood, guilt seems to be the emotion that unites all mothers, whatever their differences. It is also generated in the gap between the ideal of motherhood imposed on us by the dominant narrative and the failures that attend it in daily life. The guilt for a mother-writer is not just associated with being torn between writing and her maternal obligations; it is a tear in what one might call "identity." Motherhood requires one to be present, protective, raising citizens who can survive in our structured societies; writing, on the other hand, might require solitude, experiments, not fitting in the structures of those societies. Migration also carries within it the guilt toward those who you left behind. How would you feel while you are enjoying the mobility secured by your Canadian passport when you have friends back in Egypt who are having great difficulty obtaining visas, if not in prison or banned from travel entirely.

You're someone whose poems have been translated into many languages (French, English, Dutch, Macedonian, Hindi, Hebrew). Have you had the same kind of relationship with other translators? Do you offer any advice to translators of your work?

In the translation of my works into languages I do not know, my contribution is limited to answering the translator's questions, if any. There are two layers in written Arabic language: one of letters and the second of short vowels that also determine pronunciation and meaning but are usually omitted. Yet the absence of a single necessary short vowel in the text may cause confusion in understanding.

With English translations of my work, it has been always different since I can understand, comment, and discuss the translator choices. I used to feel anxiety about how my poems sound in English, but something changed with time. I tell myself you can't guard a poem; pretend you are a dead poet. Translation is a deep reading of a text, a translator has a voice too, and his or her choices must be respected. A poem is given a different life in a new language.

I don't have any particular advice to translators, but I

have a story. I was in grade ten or eleven when I read an Arabic translation of a short poem in the culture page of a newspaper. The poem in Arabic started, أنا لا أحد، فمن أنت؟

I'm Nobody! Who are you?

At that time, I did not know Emily Dickinson. Reading this line was an epiphany in my developing relation with poetry. The syntax of the sentence in Arabic was so odd, fresh, and unfamiliar in my reading experience. I started to be very interested in translated poetry and read some of the greatest poets available in Arabic translation. Even though some of these translations were actually bad, they were windows on different ways of writings, different traditions, experiences, and visions. The target language, Arabic in this case, is enriching itself by bringing other languages into it.

Mona Kareem published an essay a year or so back about the way in which some Western poets "kidnap" poems and do not translate them so much as "render" them as English poems (usually with the assistance of a crib or literal). The word "adaptation" or "version" is sometimes used in this regard. Do you have thoughts on this?

I fully agree with Kareem's article, "Western Poets Kidnap Your Poems and Call Them Translations." These kinds of renditions, translations, or adaptations do not bring the other writing into English but impose English language on others. They are acts of violence that happen without the necessary knowledge and facility with otherness. We can't assume that this kind of activity cares about keeping the integrity of the original voice.

Thinking of "integrity," are you suggesting that translators need to build up a relationship of trust with readers and the original text?

Yes. As Walter Benjamin wrote, "A real translation is transparent; it does not cover the original, does not block its light." If we agree that translation is a deep reading of a text, we assume that there are two languages (the original and the target language with all the specific features of each of them) and two individuals, the author and the translator. The process includes multiplicity of choices to convey this transparency as much as possible. Translation brings the original text to a new environment, readership, and interpretation. But the target language expands its vocabulary, syntax, and imagination by translating foreign texts. The adaptation of a foreign text—whatever the quality of the final product—does not create a space within its target language to welcome the foreign, because it makes itself the host and the guest.

You've had Canadian citizenship since 2007. Do you think that Canadian identity is broad enough to include your work as Canadian? Would you feel comfortable thought of as a Canadian writer?

The day I took the oath of citizenship, my younger son, who was born in Canada, was six years old. When I told him that I became Canadian today, he said, "Great, now you will stop complaining about the cold winter?" This scene can answer your question. Citizenship does not make you more Canadian, but living in Canada for twenty-four years, going through motherhood, an academic career, different writing projects, friendship, failure—these are the things that make you belong here.

I prefer not to speak of identity. Identity is a trap that dominates conversation about art and literature. Personally, I don't claim any particular identity. And Canada was not my first major move or the most influential shift. Perhaps more formative was moving from a small village to Mansoura City and then to Cairo as a young poet.

Even then, I was aware of my position as an outsider. You go through similar challenges trying to make sense of any new map or accent. Sometimes you need to be invisible. Poetry was my way of making sense of the world—in Cairo, for example. I was very much against romanticizing nature and home, and so I loved Cairo more than my ancestors' village.

In North America, I did not write any poetry for five years. I was just searching, reading lots of books, and trying to build a life in Canada.

I read lots of books that I could relate to, comparing two places: one a third world, the other a first world. These books evoke nostalgia and ask questions of identity in a particular way. However, I was not inspired to add to their number.

In Canada, I wrote about the motherhood that happens in a foreign language. I tried to understand the guilt that overwhelms me whenever I think of my privilege in ordinary things such as healthcare, freedom of speech, and mobility while I have friends back in Egypt who are prisoners or forbidden from travel.

As a migrant writer, I have always refused to become a representative of Egypt, the Arab woman, or Islam. I feel that in the literary landscape, identity is the tool used by others to classify, understand, recognize, include, or exclude you. Understanding the historical experience behind a text is very different than labels.

In your essay "Eliminating Diasporic Identities," you end on a question: "Is it possible to hide part of your history without hiding yourself?" How do you feel that Canada in particular asks you to hide parts of yourself? As opposed to, say, France or the US?

In general, my experience in Canada is different than in France or the US; it is much deeper, longer, and of course more challenging. Though Canada is a self-declared "multicultural" country, writers from elsewhere enjoy acceptance only by accepting an imposed label. When I arrived in Edmonton, I was lucky to meet some poets and writers individually through the university. They were very supportive, and we remain friends today. They kindly introduced me to the local literary scene and they presented the possibility to join it. But what I soon figured out was rather traumatizing: a writer from elsewhere, who writes in a foreign language, is reduced to some attribute of that "elsewhere," whether nation, religion, colour, geographical area, or era. This is particularly true if "elsewhere" implies an oppression—Dictatorship, Communist Totalitarianism, Patriarchy, or The Veil—for which writing provides the evidence. There is a general understanding that such an immigrant writer has escaped oppression and therefore can be defined by it in Canada. I saw this phenomenon clearly in the discourses surrounding positions such as "Writer in Exile" or "Writer in Residence," and in the ways funding is distributed to writers. There is a sense that the oppressive "elsewhere" is completely different from "here," and the role of "here"—a tolerant environment—is to provide the immigrant or refugee writer with shelter, space, sympathy, and acceptance, provided that he or she fully accepts their imposed identity label—"escapee from oppression"—and expresses that label in their writing. In this environment, diversity is more important than quality; marginalization can even become privilege.

I found this situation damaging for writers and writing—as well as for readers—and never accepted any of the possible labels (Muslim poet, Arab woman poet, etc.) offered to me, even if their rejection, ironically enough, required that I remain an outsider. I consider myself lucky to have had this awareness. Even when I was an emerging writer in Cairo, I used to mock "conscious" poetry, or praising literature for reflecting social reality or championing a social class, issue, or nation. And I reserved my profoundest mockery for any defence of "higher values" in incompetent literature, even if conforming to such literary values could convey many benefits. In Canada, the pressure to conform was even greater.

Can we end on your thoughts about the difference of process between writing poetry and prose? Is prose somehow more "predictable"? (I'm thinking of your comment on poetry being "unpredictable" above.)

The difference between poetry and prose can be seen in the process of writing. Perhaps the writer's question is more defined in prose. If you have a question about aging or motherhood, for example, you can explore, read books about it, discuss it with others, and think about it from different angles. It is as if there is room to crystallize the question, develop it, and pay attention to its shifts during writing. This was my experience in writing my two non-fiction books—*How to Mend: On Motherhood and its Ghosts* and *Traces of Enayat.* The outcome was not predictable either, but there was always room to explore, to stop, and then resume. There was also freedom to intersect different genres, where archival research, narratives, theory, memoir, fiction, and even poetry can live together in harmony.

To write a poem, it is not necessary to begin with a clear question. Maybe the poem's question is hidden, just a mood carried by language, imagination, and structure. There are so many great poems whose topics cannot even be defined.

Romanized Gauls

MICHAEL SCHMIDT

Michael Schmidt, OBE, FRSL, was born in Mexico in 1947. He studied at Harvard and at Wadham College, Oxford. He was professor of poetry at Glasgow University, where he was convenor of the creative writing programme. Founder (1969) and editorial and managing director of Carcanet Press Limited, and a founder (1972) and general editor of the literary journal *PN Review*, he has written poetry, fiction, and literary history and is a translator and anthologist. In 1998, he published *Lives of the Poets*, an epic study which connects the lives and works of over 300 English-language poets of the last 700 years. The book was a finalist for the National Book Critics Circle Award for Criticism in the US. Its notoriety in Canada stems from the fact that Canadian poetry is given very little space in its 900-plus pages and is dismissed at one point as a "short street" (repeatedly misquoted in Canadian journals as "a short street not worth going down"). Here's the damning passage in full:

> Standing at Seven Dials, we could make forays down streets called Australia, Canada (a short street, that), New Zealand, India, Ireland, South Africa, the Caribbean, the United States or Great Britain. But *English* poetry is

different from New Zealand or Caribbean poetry. New Zealand poetry may mean a great deal to the domestic readership but does not export. What interests us is poetry that is New Zealand poetry *and* English poetry. To follow *national* streets would go against the grain of this history.

For this interview, I asked Schmidt if he would like to come back to his earlier criticism, discuss whether he has changed his mind, and talk a little about how he sees Canada fitting into his new work, *The Novel: A Biography* (published in 2014). This interview was conducted between May 28 and July, 2012. Schmidt lives in Manchester, UK.

We'd better start with the "short street."

I'm afraid that when you are doing an international historical survey, a lot of local darlings get neglected because, in that context, they are invisible. *Lives of the Poets* started from a hypothesis of continuities, between poems and between poets, between seemingly discrete literatures. There are major poets who work well beyond borders, and there are those who don't. Ashbery versus Ammons, for example, or Larkin versus Betjeman. This doesn't mean that a local or national poetry is necessarily enervated or lacking in shape and even distinction; but the absence of substantial figures to appeal to a visiting reader (I was not the first to stand at Seven Dials and reach such a conclusion), with a very large wave of poetry carrying me forward from the fourteenth century, is what I was experiencing. Much as I admired Margaret Atwood as a wry presence and novelist, her poetry did not seem very good to me. Anne Carson was not at that time where she is today. Mark Strand and Elizabeth Bishop had shaken the dust of Canada off their feet. Earle Birney seemed a colossal joke, a product of Arts Council policy. I have long admired Klein, as you know.

So I was a traveller from an antique land, and I was looking for mountains or monuments or at least enormous feet of stone.

When you and Todd Swift put together your specifically Canadian anthology, I became a reader. Your anthology did not, like my critical book, come with the worlds and histories of English-language poetry at its back. Indeed, in a sense, it was about resistances to those histories and to neighbouring America (as a Mexican, I understand that) and also the alternative history of Canadian poetry that excluded the poets whose work you admired. When you focus on a limited sample of poetry from a country, with generational frames, things look different. In a room with twenty poets, some will obviously be better than others. If the judgment stays in that room and in those frames, the hills are higher, the vales are deeper. You and Todd Swift omitted a range of poets whose work I might have expected to see, poets with more greenery about them, mud on their boots, grizzlies at their backs, trailing roots and attended by livestock. But your anthology has a strangely urban and deracinated feel which I enjoy. Judging from the reviews the book has had, Canadian poetry is even more riven by factions than British, more acrimonious and ungenerous. But the anthologist, like the critic, can never expect gratitude, even from the poets included.

Much seems to begin in Canada and get absorbed into the States. That's another problem: of resource, of population, and therefore artistic density.

In any case, I enjoyed your anthology and learned from it, and yet, looking at Baxter and Curnow and Manhire in New Zealand, for instance, or Wright, Harwood, Hope and Murray in Australia, I get a sense of more seismic activity, less factionalism and factional obedience, in those literatures than in yours.

Can you say a bit more about Birney?

I think I heard him at a Poetry International back in the 1960s or early 1970s. He was the Canadian poet everyone had heard of, the one Canada promoted as the Voice of the Nation. It is possible that I enjoyed his reading. Someone, a publisher or the Canada Council, sent me a very heavy and substantial two-volume edition of his poems, hardback and boxed like a Folio Society classic. There was his "David," carried away by its sounds. The problem is that they are, many of them, especially the thick alliterations and assonances, overdone. The effect is achieved and then overwritten again and again. In this case, Poe's prescription is right about the extent of poems and the treachery of narrative when the impulse is, as I take it to be here, essentially lyrical-elegiac. There were also many poems about his travels for representing Canada. Poetry as diplomacy, poetry as outreach, poetry not as journalism—it did not have that kind of precision—but as enthusiasm, with descriptions of things or of how things affected the travelling bard. My sense was that the whole thing was too easy: the writing, the editing, the publishing, the binding, the privileging. The man was a living monument, but not like A.D. Hope, a poet of formal and thematic substance, or like James K. Baxter, a volatile genius. It didn't seem serious.

I remember hearing Bill Manhire say, roughly, that when British influence set sail never to return, New Zealand poets moved towards the Americans. In a way, Canada hasn't had that luxury. And the anti-American sentiment is as much America's fault as it is Canada's. So many draft dodgers, like Norm Sibum, brought with them and maintain negative feeling for their birthland. To whom can Canadians turn but themselves?

This is a funny argument. I wonder which precise British influence Bill was shaking off by going to the Americans, and once there, which America he adopted? This sort of language might have made sense when traditions were hegemonic, even when Bill and I were young(er), but didn't Pound and Eliot and Joyce and Lawrence rather blur these borders on maps? Canada should see America and Mexico as cultural resources: it can approach them with irony, surely, so as not to get its hands too dirty. Margaret Atwood had that wonderful open letter some time ago in which she defines, reluctantly, a distance. She does not reject but steps back. And Canada itself is hardly a hegemony. You proved that with your anthology...

I do understand the feeling a Canadian might have with so substantial and disproportionately influential a political and civic neighbour overshadowing. We Mexicans are gradually retaking the United States by means of energetic reproduction. Soon Canada, if it remains in a resistant mode, will be resisting a Greater Mexico, at which point you will experience an acute nostalgia for the days when you could claim a bit of Bellow, a bit of Bishop, a bit of Strand... and when those who weren't snared in the net of French spoke English. Spanish will be wafting across that border like fog off the Great Lakes, or the cook fires of the taco vendors...

Seriously, the demographics of Canada and the United States are now such that these arguments about unitary cultures are even more invalid than they once were... and contemporary poets seldom (*pace* Birney) subscribe to the establishment, except when it is giving them prizes and grants.

At the same time, a unitary culture—as vague and ill-defined as these things often are—can also be the defence against the overshadowing neighbour. Perhaps I'll take this opportunity to turn the conversation to Anne Carson, who for many years used a one-line bio note: "Anne Carson lives in Canada" in her American-published books. I've always read this with a touch of humility that suits Carson's humour (others see it as a ploy or perhaps cloying, which doesn't seem like her at all). But she long since abandoned it. What do you think? And where would Carson have fit in *LotP*?

I expect she said that because it meant next to nothing to her main (American) readership, to whom being a resident of Canada suggests the wilds, bears, salmon, mountains, Mounties. She wanted people to read the poems which are cosmopolitan and culturally centred and rethink the peripheries and the stereotypes. A paradox, then. I remember seeing a working girl's card in a London telephone box that made me laugh: "Fresh country girl for kinky sex." I am not comparing Anne Carson's biographical note to this, exactly, but, contrariwise, there is something odd in so complex, sophisticated, and wonderful a poet living among grizzly bears. When I was in Toronto, I was disappointed not to meet any grizzly bears, and I suspect Anne Carson may never have met one either. She is merely saying, "Rethink Canada."

In *LotP*, she would go with Moore and (somewhat less) that other Canadian, Bishop, rather than Plath or Sexton, rather than Levertov, or perhaps even more with

Niedecker and maybe even Mina Loy. Certainly, the work by her I most admire is clear-edged and classical without the enervation of HD.

The two Canadians who do appear in *LotP*, Marius Kociejowski and Norm Sibum, you connect to F.T. Prince, to wisdom as opposed to play, to the spirit. In Canada, the "wise" poets tend to connect to landscape and environment rather than myth and history (Robert Bringhurst perhaps the sole exception who attempts to connect them all). The former haven't made much of an impact outside of Canada, perhaps because landscape and environment are always local, whereas myth and history are more worldly. Carson fits in here, too, and perhaps Daryl Hine. Can you say something about this? And about Kociejowski and Sibum's connection to it?

Among the Australians, A.D. Hope was among the first to make a big impact outside Australia, and he is mythical and legendary, though there is a huge amount of Australia in his writing. (It's probably relevant to mention that he is a superb formalist also, and that tends to travel more easily than free verse.) So too with that most wonderful poet Judith Wright, whose geographies and landscapes are more and more particularly Australian until the miracle of the Ghazals, and with the abundant Les Murray, for whom the visible world—and I mean world—exists. Gwen Harwood is more your playful poet, but she too found her way at least to Britain if not to North America, because of the quality of her playfulness.

I loved Marius Kociejowski's poetry not because it was Canadian but because of his quite remarkable ear. Line by line it does amazing things, and he feels and thinks deeply and draws in the wake of his poems a huge amount of material rather than a birdless silence. Norm Sibum's work I loved not because he was Canadian, which in a sense he isn't, but because he wrote the kinds of poems I always wanted to be able to write: with big narratives, differentiated voices that were rooted in things I valued and attitudes I valued. He and I had a similar leaping-off point thanks to Vietnam; he went his way and I went— another. It seldom weighed with me where poets were from, perhaps because it did not seem to weigh with them.

I think the theory that myth and legend travel further than particularity is flawed, though. The examples of Murray and Wright, or from the New Zealand of Baxter, prove that it is probably the poets with the most world in them that travel best in a westward direction, to Britain and America. Walcott over Brathwaite, for example, because Walcott is full of world and Brathwaite is full of ideology and indignation. Or Ammons, who never crossed the ocean, as against Ashbery, who swims comfortably to and fro and belongs here with Prince and Donne and Clare as much as he belongs over there.

Canada and landscape is a bit of a problem. Canada is, like the United States, a continental country, with everything except the tropics. The poet of Saskatoon and the poet of St. John's occupy very different landscapes and, one is tempted to say, very different worlds.

What you say connects, I think, to the history I'm wondering about: Carson and Hine are classicists; Kociejowski a Londoner, a travel writer, and antiquarian bookseller; Sibum would prefer to be a Roman. And then there is Eric Ormsby, a professor of Islamic thought. You've recently published *The Baboons of Hada*, a selection of Ormsby's poems. Where do you see him as fitting into this discussion? And can you say a bit more about being "full of world"?

I regarded Eric Ormsby as, like me, a citizen of the language. Some years ago, I met him in Ireland, where I was judging a poetry competition, and I was persuaded he was an American. He got second prize. I am now persuaded he is a Greater American, like me, a NAFTA poet. We are, you will agree, talking largely about Canadian emanations. Is Sibum embraced as a Canadian? He's sort of elbowy and even prickly. How about those poets who go to rather than come from Canada and are regarded—I am thinking of Ondaatje, for example—as Canadian because they are successful. Are claimed as Canadians. Michael Ondaatje came through the Suez Canal from Sri Lanka en route to Britain and then travelled on to Canada. Looking at him as a Canadian, I wonder what he has in common with Atwood, for example: they are friends, of course. They are both great travellers. I am not sure how deep in a single place their roots go, though it is hard to think of Toronto without thinking of *In the Skin of a Lion*; but could he have written that novel had he never been outside Canada, outside English? Could he have been there if he hadn't been not there? I'd even say the same of—you.

Ormsby is free, Sibum too, and Kociejowski, partly because they don't identify with the Canada that Canada theorists construct. They have perhaps a personal rather than an ideological Canada (personal is ideological, you will say, to which the answer is yes, and no: it is specific to one and non-transferable).

If I were a French Canadian, I think I would need, profoundly, what the proponents of and apologists for Anglophone Canadian literature do not in fact need. If I were an Anglophone Canadian, I would be happy in my wide, privileged franchise. I would be concerned for the large Francophone, the Chinese, Korean, Asian, and Hispanic minorities. There is a colonial situation, but it's hard to assign conventional tags to it, not least because Britain is at best a ghostly presence, a shadow to the great United States curled up alongside.

About the Anglophone concern for "the large Franco-phone, the Chinese, Korean, Asian, and Hispanic min-orities": there's been discussion recently about the movement towards pluralism in anthologies, for instance. And perhaps in literature in general. Is this connected?

The French minority in Canada has, I believe, a developed identity which, like that of the Finnish Swedes (as before of the Finnish Finns when Swedish was the privileged language in Finland) exists in a fruitfully contra-position. It also has a real literature which rejoices in its French origins while also celebrating its differences. When I was in Toronto, it surprised me to see how enormous the other immigrant communities were, and they have grown in the twenty years since. I should mention the Caribbean minorities too, because Canada is by extension a Caribbean island, especially where poetry is concerned.

One way of getting away from an obsession with powerful neighbours and colonial antecedents is to acknowledge and resist the potentially colonial relationship between Canadian English and the older and newer literatures in other languages that coexist with it, and to make sure that colonial patterns are not repeated. Not an easy task, I appreciate, but a formal and thematic curiosity enriches Canadian writing. I think an excellent non-Canadian example is the Australian poet Judith Wright, who, towards the end of her poetry-producing life, realized she was not European and started learning lessons from Basho and from the Persian poets and produced her greatest poems by extending in those directions.

The more critically open readers become to the poetries in other languages that exist in Canada, the more critically open they will be to the diversity of Anglophone poetries that are there.

What you're arguing here reminds me of something the authors of *The Empire Writes Back* put forward back in 1989—that the Canadian cultural mosaic could generate discourses of literary hybridity to replace nationalism— which at the time wasn't the case. But in many ways Canada is now defined by the postcolonial: Rohinton Mistry, Shyam Selvadurai, Dionne Brand; even Ondaatje, who spent most of the '70s convincing everyone he is

an Anglophone rather than a postcolonial writer, has changed his tune.

But, as regards poetry, I was thinking of the pluralism William Wootten defined in the *TLS* a few months back (April 27, 2012): the way anthologies now are bigger, the way there is less a sense of one or two poets that we should all rally behind or battle against than a movement/moment we should all try and be part of. Wootten was writing about the difference between the Penguin Poets anthologies and Roddy Lumsden's *Identity Parade* (Bloodaxe, 2010), but we might also apply this to Carmine Starnino's *The New Canon* (Véhicule Press, 2006), which contains the work of fifty Canadian poets born between 1955 and 1975.

It's strange to think that before the Mexican Revolution of 1910–21, there was some poetry in Mexico, epitomized in the work of Ramon Lopez Velarde, for example, which had much in common with Laforgue's poetry, and Guido Gozzano's, and early Eliot's—and was no less Mexican in inflection for that. All these poets, from different parts of the world, were participating in a "moment." It didn't last, but while it did, Velarde was aware of Europe, especially of France and what was going on there, an awareness not imitative but resourceful. Mexican in inflection does not mean Mexican by design; that is, Lopez Velarde was not affirming anything, Zacatecas happened to be in Mexico and its air he breathed. Hybridity nowadays is deliberate, a matter of choice and design, treating the genetic chain like rosary beads. Formal choices seem often to be preceded by political calculations. Nationalism is not a necessity. It emerges at times of revolution and struggled-for independence. If there has not been a physical struggle, it can be much harder to get it off the ground. After the Revolution in Mexico, people started writing Mexican Poetry and for a time stopped writing poetry. In Dublin, as a young man, Joyce was momentously exposed to Ibsen's plays in performance; after Irish independence, Ibsen was out of bounds for decades while an Irish theatre emerged. Gains—and losses. Making literature instrumental, whatever the gains, from my perspective, always entails a profound and durable loss, unless the poet is Whitman, say, but there is only Whitman, and the instrumentality there was prophetic and visionary, broadening and eventually inclusive.

It is a convenient fashion to be postcolonial. Even a major writer like Wole Soyinka at Poetry Parnassus this month was talking about how he uses certain terms and themes because they are understood, not because they are endemic or necessary to him.

You mention anthologies, a subject dear to my heart. Anthologies of poetry needn't be indiscriminate. They may be bigger because the anthologist rebels against the Golden Treasury approach and feels that if a poet is worth including, s/he is worth reading in extenso. For my part, I subscribe, as a reader and as an editor, to Thom Gunn's "spectrum" argument, which he proposed eloquently in an essay in *PN Review*, demonstrating a continuity in American poetry from the work of Edgar Bowers at one extreme to that of Michael Palmer at the other, with gradations between. It is this sense not of oppositions, cliques, encampments, or interest groups but of contiguous and interdependent strata. It's the sort of approach that leads to Starnino's kind of anthology (which I do find a little too optimistic in its harvest of fifty poets from two decades but still compelling in its intelligence), but not to Lumsden's. There are borders, of course, but they are permeable. Note that Starnino's title proposes a canon, which implies the creation of a diverse, common, and authoritative poetry; Lumsden's proposes a triumphal parade of discreet identities, marching obediently forward. A generational victory parade.

Big question before we move on to *The Novel: A Biography*. Almost fifteen years after *LotP*, do you think Canada has moved beyond the short street? Would you change your assessment in an update? Which poets might you add?

I would add Anne Carson, for sure, and Klein. I enjoy P.K. Page—your anthology brought her and others into focus for me—Richard Outram; Eric Ormsby, who has strayed onto the Carcanet list; Dionne Brand, whose work you and Kei Miller, from very different geographies, brought to my attention (and the fact that she cannot be appropriated is to her credit: A.F. Moritz, Elise Partridge, Marius Kociejowski, Robyn Sarah, Norm Sibum, and quite a few others in your book are in a similarly ambiguous position). Many of the poets in your anthology are arresting. If I was to be revising *LotP*, of course, I would be under various constraints, not least that of space, and I am not sure how long the comparative street would be, or how Canadian with a capital C it could be given that so many Canadian poets are Canadian more because of the deliberate erasure of another nationality, or by nurture, not nature… I wonder how many Canadian poets insist on Canadianness and how many are marshalled into that category by those who want to consolidate the notion of a distinctive and definable Canadian poetry?

Certainly, there was a generation who insisted on Canadianness, on defining and identifying it against at times both the American and the British. You won't find any of those poets in our anthology. But then Al Moritz has admitted to me that his leaving the US had to do with a revulsion towards American politics in the early '70s—though never its literature and art. So he walked away from one side of America. That revulsion was the spirit of a Canadian age in many ways. But that age is on its way out. Perhaps what happened had to happen. But we are no longer the polite, radical liberals with a socialist agenda that American comedians mock us as. Our current conservative leader is in the *Guardian* just today (July 9, 2012) making a mess of the environmental sciences, having already pulled Canada out of the Kyoto Accord. Canada's braggadocio—its success, its ripe resources in an age of depletion—is dangerous. It is ballsiness and egocentricity. It is the Griffin Prize. Look what we can do with our money (don't forget we're Canadian)! Will you share your thoughts on prize culture? And the Griffin?

The Griffin Prize always seemed to me a great and good award. It acknowledged the international and placed a Canadian each year on the big stage. But on the whole, prize culture, like performance culture, seems to me a distorting thing. Many poets can't perform, and most poets don't win prizes. The creation of a culture of plausibility becomes restrictive. The fruits are obedience, writers writing for toffee apples, as in fiction, where the presence of the big screen and its rewards actually impacted on the pacing and texturing of novels. Odd how many novelists, for two long generations, made some of their money from script writing, and the lucky ones from film deals.

Performance and prize culture are aspects of the commodification of poetry and the dumbing down, the decorum of relevance and accessibility.

How does Canada fare in *The Novel: A Biography?*

Now that would be breaking an embargo! I can tell you that Saul Bellow is one of my cynosures. Is Malcolm Lowry Canadian, if Michael Ondaatje is, and Rohinton Mistry? Does mentioning Bellow help? There are an awful lot of novelists included in the book, and some of them are Canadian. I introduce the subject with a paragraph that runs something like, "Although each year Margaret Atwood is named as a contender, the emergence of Canadian literature has yet to be marked by the award of a Nobel Prize, unless we count Saul Bellow who was born in Lachine, Quebec but emigrated with his already emigrant parents to Chicago when he was nine." Canada's proximity to the United States and its colonial British legacies, complicated by the French, make the postcolonial situation exasperating for Canadian writers keen to assert and theorize their otherness. The desire not to be rolled into American literature and at the same time to affirm the distance of an ocean from the colonial grandmamma survives. Canada possesses substantial, distinctive novelists, born and adoptive, and a literary scene as savage and political as any in the world.

There follows an account of Robertson Davies (your Victor Hugo) and Michael Ondaatje, whose *In the Skin of a Lion* I thought most original in lots of ways, *The Cat's Table* by miles the least. In a later chapter, Margaret Atwood features. I was interested to see what an impact Frye had had on her, and perhaps, through her, on other Canadian writers, trying to establish difference. Her *Survival: A Thematic Guide to Canadian Literature* laid Fryesque foundations, and *Strange Things: The Malevolent North in Canadian Literature* is a compelling reconception.

Frye was himself keen to define Canadian writing and in the end seemed to think, as Atwood did for a time, perhaps still, that it could be characterized in terms of its themes: a fear of nature, the history of colonization and settlement (the majority voice as colonizers and settlers and dispossessors), and a binding sense of community. For him, these characteristics were not static and might develop. But in terms of forms, in terms of differentiations of language, not much, so that a lot of American—in the sense of United States—writing, especially perhaps from the south, is Canadian. The categories so far drawn are not in the end specific enough, maybe, to fit the baggy map?

There is a moment where something wonderful happens out of something dreadful. Atwood's sense of the United States as a political, economic, and above all cultural power came to a head in April 2003, when she published the long-meditated "A Letter to America" defining, at the start of the Iraq War, the difference of the United States, rather than the difference of Canada. That was really radical. It felt to her that the United States was sliding down the incline towards the dystopian Republic of Gilead she created in *The Handmaid's Tale.* So she begins, "Dear America: This is a difficult letter to write, because I'm no longer sure who you are." That "you" had almost become a "we" or a "me," so much culture was shared; "you were the amazing trio, Hemingway, Fitzgerald, and Faulkner, who traced the dark labyrinths of your hidden heart. You were Sinclair Lewis and Arthur Miller, who, with their own American idealism, went after the sham in you, because they thought you could do better." And "you" couldn't. She lays out the evidence. "You put God on the money, though, even then. You had a way of thinking that the things of Caesar were the same as the things of God: that gave you self-confidence. You have always wanted to be a city upon a hill, a light to all nations, and for a while you were." The Canadians are the Romanized Gauls, looking over the wall at the real Romans. And what do they see? Apart from the invasion of Iraq, "You're gutting the Constitution. [...] You're running up a record level of debt. [...] You're torching the American economy." The consequences are enumerated. She enjoins them to summon their sleeping patriots, "Summon them now, to stand with you, to inspire you, to defend the best in you. You need them." It is a boldly polemical sermon-letter. An oblique and decisive declaration of independence. The "I" who speaks it, though—will Canada ever be that "I"?

ACKNOWLEDGEMENTS

A number of these interviews appeared in magazines or online over the years: *Arc* (Sarah), *Canadian Notes & Queries* (Moritz, Schmidt), *Manchester Review* (Coles, Bringhurst, Compton), *Partisan* (Heighton), *PN Review* (Hine, Sibum, Kociejowski, Matuk), and *Puritan* (Partridge).

I am grateful to Michael Schmidt, for enabling my interview habit in the early days, and to all of the poets who responded and took time to work with me.